Richard Nicholls Worth

The West Country Garland

Selected from the Writings of the Poets of Devon and Cornwall

Richard Nicholls Worth

The West Country Garland
Selected from the Writings of the Poets of Devon and Cornwall

ISBN/EAN: 9783337007300

Printed in Europe, USA, Canada, Australia, Japan

Cover: Foto ©ninafisch / pixelio.de

More available books at **www.hansebooks.com**

THE

West Country Garland:

SELECTED FROM THE WRITINGS OF THE POETS
OF DEVON AND CORNWALL,

FROM THE FIFTEENTH TO THE NINETEENTH CENTURY,

WITH

Folk Songs and Traditional Verses.

BY

R. N. WORTH, F.G.S.,

*Author of "The History of Plymouth," "The History of Devonport,"
"The Three Towns' Bibliotheca," "Historical Notes concerning
the Progress of Mining Skill in Cornwall and Devon,"
&c. &c.*

"The inventory
Of your best graces."—*Shakspere, Henry VIII.*

LONDON:
HOULSTON & SONS, 7, PATERNOSTER BUILDINGS
PLYMOUTH: W. BRENDON & SON.
1875.

INTRODUCTION.

THE *West Country Garland* contains examples of the writings of nearly a hundred poets of varying merit connected with the Two Counties of Devon and Cornwall. At least twice that number of local poetic writers might have been quoted without descending below the level of mediocrity; but the object of the *Garland* is to illustrate, not to exhaust; to indicate the high value of Western poetic writers, not to give a complete list either of names or of examples. And I venture to think that the selection now offered to the public will sustain the claims of the district whence it springs to a leading place in the poetic literature of the country. Indeed, when two or three great names are excepted, it may fairly be asserted that no county in England has greater reason to be proud of its poets than Devon.

The arrangement of the *Garland* is in the main, so far as the authors are concerned, chronological.

Certain anonymous poems, the dates of which are known, are placed in order accordingly; while at the end of the collection will be found various traditional pieces—some of great antiquity—which have retained their currency.

The work of selection, alike of authors and of poems, has been attended with some difficulties and no little trouble. Many pieces of considerable merit are yet, from their length or from other causes, ill-adapted for quotation; and in this way what would perhaps be the best examples of several authors have of necessity been excluded. On the other hand, it not unfrequently happens that writers of inferior general standing do now and then rise very far above their ordinary level. The selections must not therefore be regarded as in all cases conclusive of the merits of the writers quoted.

Moreover, the standard of poetic excellence has varied greatly. There are poets, considered as of the greatest excellence in their day, who have now deservedly passed into oblivion: there are others, whose merits it has been reserved almost for the present age to recognize. I have thought it desirable, within the limits assigned, to make the *Garland* as complete a reflection of the poetic mind of the West as possible. This will account for the inclusion of a few pieces less from their interest and value as poetry, than because they illustrate a style of writing once highly in favour; or are the work of writers who in their day were held in the world's esteem, but have now descended from their high estate.

The quotations cover a space of nearly four centuries, and it is hoped may have some value as an illustration, not local merely, of the literary history of the kingdom during that period. I have purposely kept my citations from living writers within very narrow limits. There never was a time when the faculty for verse-making was so general, and when there were so many who "write with ease," and frequently with no little poetic feeling. To have extended the *Garland* beyond its present limits in this direction would, however, have involved an amount of criticism foreign to its purpose, and would hardly have tended to advance the object for which it was compiled.

Those who wish to make acquaintance with the poets and rhymers of the West beyond that to which this little volume will afford a key, may easily do so. The *Bibliotheca Cornubiensis* of Messrs. G. C. Boase and W. P. Courtney, now publishing, contains as full an account of the writers of this class who are connected with the county of Cornwall as it is possible to procure. It is all-inclusive, even of the most fugitive and ephemeral productions; and when finished will be the most complete *Bibliotheca* in existence. For the sister county the *Bibliotheca Devoniensis* of Mr. Davidson may be consulted, though it is very far indeed from full; and for the district of Plymouth, Devonport, and Stonehouse, my own *Three Towns' Bibliotheca*. But special reference is due to the account of the Devonshire poets which has been undertaken by Mr. J. R. Chanter, of Barnstaple, the first part of which appeared in the *Transactions* for 1874 of the Devonshire Association for the Promotion of Science, Literature, and Art.

The materials for a sketch of the history of poetry in the West of England prior to the beginning of the 16th century are very scanty. Doubtless the Britons of Danmonia had their bards, like the Cymry of Wales; but we know nothing of them; and it is very doubtful, Tintagel notwithstanding, how far the legends of King Arthur can be traced back to a purely Western source, though assuredly some fragments at least we may claim. In Anglo-Saxon times, and indeed after Athelstan had conquered the West, the whole of Cornwall and part of Devon still remained in British hands, and the amount of Saxon influence was comparatively small. Leofric, the first bishop of Exeter, installed personally in that see by Edward the Confessor and his Queen, gave to the Chapter Library of the Cathedral a large book of Anglo-Saxon poetry, which is now known as the *Codex Exoniensis*, and has been published under the editorship of Mr. Thorpe. It is quite within the bounds of possibility that a county which produced Boniface, the Apostle of Germany, should have had its poets as well as its preachers; and it is highly probable that some of the pieces in the Exeter *Codex* may have been the production of local writers. But this is only a suggestion at the best.

The first poets recorded as belonging to the district are Josephus Iscanus, or Joseph of Exeter, and Michael Blaumpinus, or Blaumpayne, a native of Cornwall; who flourished in the 12th and 13th centuries. They both wrote in Latin; and the first had the honour of producing, in his *De Bello Trojano*, the very finest of all the mediæval Anglo-Latin poems. Such indeed is its merit, that it passed under the name of Cornelius Nepos. Of Michael of Cornwall's "Rhymes for merry England" Camden writes in terms of praise. He had a turn for epigrams; but was far inferior to Iscanus. Much about the same date as this, Hugh of Rutland settled in Cornwall, and wrote a couple of romances in Anglo-Norman. Camden makes several quotations from the *Architrenium* of John Havillan, another Cornish writer of Latin verse.

The remainder of the thirteenth, the fourteenth, and the greater part of the fifteenth centuries appear to have been absolutely barren of Western poets; and the first local poetic writer in the vernacular of whom we have any record is Alexander Barclay, with a quotation from whose quaint *Shippe of Foolis* the

Garland commences. It is not, however, until the latter half of the 16th century that the West makes its mark; but the poets whom it then sent forth were worthy of its heroes, and may almost share with them the glory of having made Devon the foremost county of England in the great days of Elizabeth. There is no need to do more than mention the names of Sir Walter Raleigh, Humphry Gifford, George Peele, and John Ford, the two last by no means the least celebrated of the Elizabethan dramatists.

The next half century was little inferior. It produced Thomas Carew, of Devonshire descent, a favourite poet of his day; William Browne, whose Pastorals, in the Spenserian style, are worthy of his master; Sidney Godolphin, whose amatory pieces deserve to be far more widely known than they are. To the latter end of the century we owe the only poet laureate (not by any means its chief matter of pride) to whom the West can lay claim—Nicholas Rowe, more worthy of note as the first editor of Shakspere; Tom D'Urfey, the prolific; and a far greater name, John Gay. With the latter exception, the West had little part in the so-called Augustan age of English literature, though the influences of that time are very plainly manifested in our minor poets of the last century, who are far better examples of style and finish than of poetic spirit. In this respect they contrast unfavourably with our lesser writers of almost every other period, the average excellence of whom is exceptionally high.

The last half of the eighteenth century, however, was so far from unfruitful that—the corresponding part of the fifteenth excepted—it is the period of which Devon has most reason to be proud. It produced John Wolcott, better known as Peter Pindar, whose almost unequalled powers of rough satire drew down upon him the fierce invective of his contemporary and fellow-Devonian, Gifford. It produced Carrington, who as a descriptive writer has no superior in the second rank of English poets; Coleridge, Devon's greatest name; and Sir John Bowring, a true poet himself, and the author of translations from the poetry of more foreign languages than any other Englishman.

Nor has the nineteenth century been far behind. We owe to it such names as Praed, the first master of society verse; Kingsley, whose recent loss we so much deplore; besides writers yet living who worthily maintain the old reputation.

Enough has now been said to indicate how great is the poetic wealth of Devon and Cornwall, so rich in worthies of all kinds—statesmen, divines, soldiers, sailors, discoverers, men of science, historians, and artists, as well as poets. Hitherto the last have been the least fully recognised. It is my hope that these pages may have their use in removing this reproach; and that while they will be found of interest in themselves, they may prove—in some cases at least—but the stepping-stone to a more enlarged acquaintance with a body of writers so well-deserving.

I have only, in conclusion, to tender my thanks to gentlemen who have kindly rendered me aid, and especially to Mr. R. J. King and Mr. J. Shelly; also to the Rev. R. S. Hawker, Mr. N. Michell, Mr. H. S. Stokes, Mr. Mortimer Collins, and Mr. E. Capern, for their courtesy in permitting quotations from their works.

CONTENTS.

	Page
B., R. R.—	
Impromptu Bruneliana	156
BAIRD, HENRY—	
Girt Ofvenders an' Zmal	152
BAMPFYLDE, JOHN—	
On a Wet Summer	70
BARCLAY, ALEXANDER—	
The Bookworm	1
BIDLAKE, JOHN—	
Descriptions of Devonshire Scenery	67
BOWRING, SIR JOHN—	
Coplas de Jorge Manrique	100
BRAY, E. A.—	
To the Tavy	84
BRETT, LYNE—	
The Sea	63
BROWNE, WILLIAM—	
Lydford Law	29
To Devon	34
BULTEEL, JOHN—	
To Chloris	54
CAPERN, EDWARD—	
Where hast thou been, my beautiful Spring?	150

CAREW, RICHARD—
  My Fishful pond is my delight . . . 15
  The Well of St. Keyne 16
CAREW, THOMAS—
  Disdain returned 28
CARRINGTON, N. T.—
  Dartmoor 78
CHEARE, ABRAHAM—
  Verses Written on the Wall of his Prison . . 45
CHORLEY, C.—
  What constitutes a Mine 132
COLERIDGE, S. T.—
  Love 74
COLLINS, MORTIMER—
  River of Dart 148
DANIEL, ALEXANDER—
  An Invocation 39
DAVY, SIR HUMPHRY—
  St. Michael's Mount . . . 85
  The Land's End 86
DIXON, SOPHIE—
  The Voice of Nature . . . 128
DOWNE, JOHN—
  The Christian's Answer to the Epicure . . . 19
DRAYTON, MICHAEL—
  The Combat of Corinæus and Goemagot . . 17
DREWE, E. A.—
  The Half-peeled Turnip 90
D'URFEY, TOM—
  The Trimmer 47
EMETT—
  To the Lark on Dartmoor . . . 94
FITZ-GEOFFRY, C.—
  Sir Francis Drake's Choice 20

CONTENTS.

FORD, JOHN—
    A Dirge 21
    Vanitas Vanitatum 21
    Atheism 22
    Description of Hell . . . 23
    The Voyage of Life . . 24
    Death 24

GAY, JOHN—
    Sweet William's Farewell to Black-eyed Susan . . 59

GIBBONS, ANNE—
    St. Peter's Day at Polperro . . . 156

GIFFORD, HUMPHRY—
    For a Gentlewoman 5

GIFFORD, WILLIAM—
    To Peter Pindar 71

GILBERT, DAVIES—
    Cornish Nonsense Verses 88

GODOLPHIN, SIDNEY—
    Constant Love 43

GRENFIELD, HENRY—
    Hymnus Vespertinus 55

GRENVILLE, Sir RICHARD—
    Sir Richard Grenville's Farewell . . 3

HATFIELD, S. E.—
    A Wish 141

HAWKER, R. S.—
    Trelawny, or the Song of the Western Men . . 139

HERRICK, ROBERT—
    Farewell to Deanbourne . . . 34

HICKS, W. R.—
    Epigrams 129

HINGSTON, FRANCIS—
    Oh, keep thy songs for me 110

HOWARD, NATHANIEL—
    To a Swallow 109

JACKSON, G. F.—
  Resurgam 134
JOHNS—
  Gaveston on Dartmoor 122
JOHNS, H. I.—
  To Evening 128
KENDALL, WILLIAM—
  To Laura 85
KILLIGREW, HENRY—
  Song 46
KINGSLEY, CHARLES—
  Ode to the North-east Wind 136
KITTO, JOHN—
  Alternatives 118
LANSDOWNE, LORD
  Love 62
LE GRICE—
  Cornish Nonsense Verses 89
LLEWELLIN, MARTIN—
  Sir Bevill Grenville 53
LUCK, R.—
  The Visiting Lady 58
MARRIOTT, J.—
  Marriage is like a Devonshire Lane . . . 97
MICHELL, NICHOLAS—
  Tintagel 146
NORTHCOTE, JAMES—
  The Hare and the Bramble 66
PEELE, GEORGE—
  A Farewell to the Famous and Fortunate Generals
    of our English Forces 12
PRAED, W. M.—
  The Chant of the Brazen Head . . . 111
  A New Ballad 115

CONTENTS.

	Page
POLWHELE, JOHN—	
Sir John Eliot	53
POLWHELE, RICHARD—	
Winter	73
PROWSE, W. J.—	
Tramp Song	131
RALEIGH, SIR WALTER—	
The Nymph's Reply to the Passionate Shepherd	8
The Country's Recreations	10
ROWE, NICHOLAS—	
The Visit	58
SMITH, JAMES—	
Oberon's Wardrobe	41
SPRAT, THOMAS—	
The Lord Protector Cromwell	49
STEVENS, J.—	
Memory	119
STOKES, H. S.—	
The Lady of Place	141
STRODE, WILLIAM—	
Plymouth in 1625	37
SWETE, JOHN—	
All for the Best	95
THOMSON—	
Dolly Pentreath's Epitaph	86
TOZER, ELIAS—	
The Resurrection and the Life	130
TREGELLAS, J. T.—	
Grammer's Cat and Ours	153
WOLCOTT, JOHN—	
The Apple Dumplings and a King	64
Epigram	66
WESLEY, SAMUEL—	
Song	61

CONTENTS.

TRADITIONAL AND ANONYMOUS—

	Page
Perseverance	8
Sir Francis Drake ; or, Eighty-eight	25
Sir Francis Drake and Queen Elizabeth	27
Inscription on Bulmer's Silver Cup	35
Inscription under a Portrait of Drake belonging to the Plymouth Corporation	36
Song in Old Cornish	87
St. Aubyn Election Song	98
The Ride to Sea	120
Helston Furry-day Song	157
Padstow Hobby-horse Songs	159
Sir John Barleycorn	165
The Barley Mow Song	167
The Cuckoo	168
The Press-gang	169
The Chapter of Admirals	174

THE
WEST COUNTRY GARLAND.

The Bookworm.

ALEXANDER BARCLAY (*circa* 1480-1552) appears to have been a Devonshire man, though there is some doubt as to his nativity. He was at one time a priest or prebend of the college of St. Mary Ottery. His chief work is the *Shippe of Foolis*, published in 1508, which may be described as a paraphrase of a translation of Sebastian Brandt's *Ship of Fools*, written in 1494. The Bookworm might with greater propriety be called the Bookman now. The satire is as applicable as ever.

THAT in this ship the chiefe place I governe,
By this wide sea with foolis wandering,
The cause is plain, and easy to discerne;
Still am I busy bookes assembling.
For to have plenty it is a pleasaunt thing,
In my conceyt to have them ay in hand;
But what they meane do I not understande.

But yet I have them in great reverence
And honour, saving them from filth and ordure
By often brusshing and much diligence,
Full goodly bounde in pleasaunt coverture
Of damas sattin, or els of velvet pure :
I keepe them sure, fearing least they should be lost ;
For in them is the cunning wherein I me boast.

But if it fortune that any learned men
Within my house fall to disputation,
I draw the curtaynes to show my bookes then,
That they of my cunning should make probation :
I love not to fall in altercation :
And while the commen, my bookes I turne and winde ;
For all is in them, and nothing in my minde.

Ptolemeus the riche caused longe agone,
Over all the worlde good bookes to be sought.
Done was this commandement.

*　　*　　*　　*　　*　　*

So in likewise of bookes I have store ;
But few I reade, and fewer understande ;
I folowe not their doctrine nor their lore—
It is enough to bear a booke in hande :
It were too much to be in such a lande
For to be bounde to loke within the booke,
I am content on the fayre coverying to looke.

Eche is not lettered that nowe is made a lorde,
Nor eche a clerke that hath a benefice ;
They are not all lawyers that plees do recorde ;
All that are promoted are not fully wise ;
On suche a chance now fortune throwes her dice ;
That though one knowe but the yrishe game,
Yet would he have a gentleman's name.

So in likewise I am in such a case,
Though I nought can,* I would be called wise ;
Also I may set another in my place,
Which may for me my bookes exercise ;
Or els I will ensue the common guise,
And say *concedo* to every argument,
Lest by much speech my Latin should be spent.

Sir Richard Grenville's Farewell.

THIS piece is also entitled—" In praise of seafaring men in hope of good fortune, and describing evil fortune." It is in the Add. MSS., British Museum, 2497, Art. 9. The author was Sir Richard Grenville, who died in 1550. He must not be confounded with his famous kinsman, Sir Richard Grenville, who died, in 1591, of wounds received in an action, which he sustained in one ship—the *Revenge*—single-handed for fifteen hours, against a Spanish fleet of 53 vessels, four of which he sunk, and others seriously injured. His crew numbered only 143 men, while the Spaniards

* Know.

had 10,000, of whom more than a thousand were lost. The *Revenge* herself sank after the action. The old spelling is retained in the first stanza.

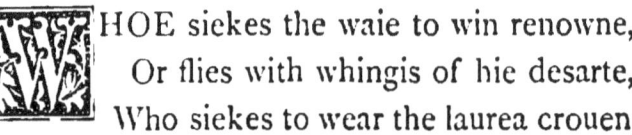HOE siekes the waie to win renowne,
  Or flies with whingis of hie desarte,
    Who siekes to wear the laurea crouen,
  Or hath the mind that would espire—
Lett him his native soylle eschew,
Lett him go rainge and seeke a newe.

Each haughty heart is well content
  With every chance that shall betide—
No hap can hinder his intent;
  He steadfast stands though fortune slide.
The sun, quoth he, doth shine as well
Abroad as erst where I did dwell.

In change of streams each fish can live;
  Each fowl content with every air;
Each haughty heart remaineth still,
  And not be drowned in deep despair;
Wherefore I judge all lands alike
To haughty hearts who fortune seek.

To pass the seas some think a toil;
  Some think it strange abroad to roam;
Some think it grief to leave their soil,
  Their parents, kinsfolk, and their home.
Think so who list, I like it not;
I must abroad to try my lot.

Who list at home at cart to drudge,
　　And cark and care for worldly trash,
With buckled shoes let him go trudge,
　　Instead of lance a whip to slash;
A mind that base his kind will show
Of carrion sweet to feed a crow.

If Jason of that mind had been,
　　The Grecians, when they came to Troy,
Had never so the Trojans foiled,
　　Nor ne'er put them to such annoy;
Wherefore who list to live at home,
To purchase fame I will go roam.

For a Gentlewoman.

HUMPHRY GIFFORD, "of the Poultry Compter, London, gent.," was of the Devonshire family of that name, settled at Halesbury, in the North of Devon. His poems were published in 1580 under the quaint title of a *Posie of Gilloflowers*, and have been reprinted in the miscellanies of the Fuller Worthies Library.

LIKE as a forte or fencèd towne,
　　By foes assault that lies in field,
When bulwarkes all are beaten downe
　　Is by perforce constraynde to yeelde:
So I that could no while withstand
　　The battery of your pleasant love,
The flagge of truce tooke in my hande
　　And meant your mercy for to prove.

My foolish fancie did enforce
    Me first to like your friendly sute,
Whiles your demands bred such remorce,
    That I coulde not the same refute.
I bad you take with free consent
    All that which true pretence did crave,
And you remaynde as one content
    The thing obtayned that you would have.
Such friendly lookes and countenance fayre,
    You freely then to me profest,
As if all troth that ever were
    Had harboured beene within your breast.
And I which saw such perfect shewes
    Of fraudlesse fayth in you appeare,
Did yeelde myselfe to Cupid's lawes,
    And shewde likewise a merrie cheere;
No loving toyes I did withholde,
    And no suspect did make me doubt:
Till your demeanure did vnfolde
    The wileé traines ye went about.
Who sees a ruinous house to fall,
    And will not shift to get him thence,
When limmes be crusht, and broken all,
    It's then too late to make defence.
When pleasant bait is swallowed downe,
    The hooked fish is sure to die:
On these Dame Fortune oft doe frowne,
    As trust too farre before they trie.

FOR A GENTLEWOMAN.

Oft had I wist, who makes his moane,
    It's ten to one he never thrives;
When thieves are from the gibbet throwne
    No pardon then can save their lives:
Such good advice as comes too late,
    May well be calde Sir Fore Wit's foole;
Elswhere goe play the cosening mate,
    I am not now to goe to schoole;
But cleerely doe at length discerne
    The marke to which my bow is bent;
And these examples shall me warne,
    What harme they have that late repent.
Your sugred speech was but a baite,
    Wherwith to bleare my simple eyes;
And vnder these did lurke deceipt,
    As poison vnder hony lies.
Wherefore since now your drift is knowne,
    Goe set your staule some other where:
I may not be so overthrowne;
    Your double dealings make me feare.
When steede by thieves is stolne away,
    I will not then the doore locke fast;
Wherfore depart without delay,
    Your words are winde, your sute is wast;
And this shalbe the final doome
    That I to your request will give,
Your love in me shall have no roome,
    Whiles life and breath shall make me live.

Perseverance.

ONE of a series of ancient inscriptions on panels in Pengwersick Castle, near Helston.

WHAT thing is harder than a rock?
What softer is than water clear?
Yet will the same, with often drop,
The hard rock pierce, as doth appear:
Even so, nothing so hard to attayne
But may be had with labour and payne.

The Nymph's Reply to the Passionate Shepherd.

SIR WALTER RALEIGH (1552-1618) was born at Hayes, near Budleigh Salterton, in Devonshire. Statesman, philosopher, courtier, gallant soldier, daring sailor; he was also a true poet. Witness this reply to Marlow's "Come, live with me, and be my love."

IF all the world and love were young,
And truth in every shepherd's tongue,
These pretty pleasures might me move
To live with thee and be thy love.

Time drives the flocks from field to field,
When rivers rage and rocks grow cold;
And Philomel becometh dumb,
And age complains of cares to come.

The flowers do fade, and wanton fields
To wayward winter reckoning yields;
A honey tongue, a heart of gall,
Is fancy's spring, but sorrow's fall.

Thy gowns, thy shoes, thy beds of roses,
Thy cap, thy kirtle, and thy posies,
Soon break, soon wither, soon forgotten,
In folly ripe, in reason rotten.

Thy belt of straw, with ivy buds,
Thy coral clasps, and amber studs;
All these in me no means can move
To come to thee and be thy love.

Why should we talk of dainties then—
Of better meat than fits for men?
These are but vain; that's only good
Which God hath blessed and sent for food.

But could youth last, and love still breed,
Had joys no date, nor age no need,
Then these delights my mind might move
To live with thee and be thy love.

The Country's Recreations.

RALEIGH.

UIVERING fears, heart-tearing cares,
Anxious sighs, untimely tears,
   Fly, fly to courts,
   Fly to fond worldings' sports,
Where trained sardonic smiles are glowing still,
And Grief is forced to laugh against her will.

Fly from our country's pastimes, fly,
Sad troops of human misery.
   Come, serene looks,
   Clear as the crystal brooks,
Or the pure azure heaven that smiles to see
The rich attendance on our poverty;
   Peace and a secure mind,
   Which all men seek, we only find.

Abused mortals, did you know
Where joy, heart's ease, and comforts grow,
   You'd scorn proud towers,
   And seek them in those bowers;
Where winds sometimes our woods may shake,
But blustering care could never tempest make;
   Nor murmurs e'er come nigh us,
   Saving of fountains that glide by us.

Here's no fantastic masque or dance,
But of our kids that frisk and prance;
    Nor wars are seen,
    Unless upon the green
Two harmless lambs are butting one the other,
Which done, both bleating run each to his mother;
    And wounds are never found,
    Save what the ploughshare gives the ground.

Here are no entrapping baits
To hasten to too hasty fates,
    Unless it be
    The fond credulity
Of silly fish, which, worldling-like, still look
Upon the bait, but never on the hook:
    Nor envy, 'less among
    The birds for prize of their sweet song.

Go, let the diving negro seek
For gems hid in some forlorn creek:
    We all pearls scorn,
    Save what the dewy morn
Congeals upon each little spire of grass,
Which careless shepherds beat down as they pass:
    And gold ne'er here appears,
    Save what the yellow Ceres bears.

Blest silent groves, oh may you be
For ever mirth's best nursery!

May pure contents
For ever pitch their tents [mountains:
Upon these downs, these meads, these rocks, these
And peace still slumber by these purling fountains:
Which we may every year
Meet when we come a-fishing here.

A Farewell,

ENTITLED, TO THE FAMOUS AND FORTUNATE GENERALS OF
OUR ENGLISH FORCES, ETC. 1589.

GEORGE PEELE (1553-1597), born in Devonshire, dramatist.

AVE done with care, my hearts! aboard amain
With stretching sails to plough the swelling
waves:
Bid England's shore and Albion's chalky cliffs
Farewell; bid stately Troynovant adieu,
Where pleasant Thames from Isis' silver head
Begins her quiet glide, and runs along
To that brave bridge, the bar that thwarts her course,
Near neighbour to the ancient stony Tower—
The glorious hold that Julius Cæsar built.
Change love for arms; girt to your blades, my boys!
Your rests and muskets take, take helm and targe,
And let God Mars his consort make you mirth—
The roaring cannon and the brazen trump,
The angry-sounding drum, the whistling fife,

The shrieks of men, the princely courser's neigh.
Now vail your bonnets to your friends at home:
Bid all the lovely British dames adieu,
That under many a standard well advanced
Have hid the sweet alarms and braves of love.
Bid theatres and proud tragedians,
Bid Mahomet, Scipio, and mighty Tamburlaine,
King Charlemagne, Tom Stukely, and the rest
Adieu. To arms, to arms, to glorious arms!
With noble Norris and victorious Drake,
Under the sanguine cross—brave England's badge
To propagate religious piety—
And hew a passage with your conquering swords
By land and sea, wherever Phœbus' eye,
Th' eternal lamp of heaven, lends us light:
By golden Tagus or the Western Inde,
Or through the spacious bay of Portugal,
The wealthy ocean main, the Tyrrhene sea,
From great Alcides' pillars branching forth,
Even to the gulf that leads to lofty Rome;
There to deface the spoils of Antichrist,
And pull his paper walls and Popery down—
A famous enterprise for England's strength:
To steel your swords on Avarice' triple crown,
And cleanse Augeas' stalls in Italy.
To arms, my fellow-soldiers! Sea and land
Lie open to the voyage you intend;
And sea or land, bold Britons, far or near,

Whatever course your matchless virtue shapes,
Whether to Europe's bounds or Asian plains,
To Afric's shore or rich America,
Down to the shades of deep Avernus' crags.
Sail on, pursue your honours to your graves ;
Heaven is a sacred covering for your heads,
And every climate virtue's tabernacle.
To arms, to arms, to honourable arms !
Hoist sails, weigh anchors up, plough up the seas
With flying keels, plough up the land with swords :
In God's name venture on : and let me say
To you, my mates, as Cæsar said to his,
Striving with Neptune's hills : "You bear," quoth he,
"Cæsar and Cæsar's fortunes in your ships."
You follow them whose swords successful are :
You follow Drake, by sea the scourge of Spain,
The dreadful Dragon, terror to your foes,
Victorious in his return from Inde,
In all his high attempts unvanquished ;
You follow noble Norris, whose renown,
Won in the fertile fields of Belgia,
Spreads by the gates of Europe to the courts
Of Christian kings and heathen potentates.
You fight for Christ and England's peerless Queen—
Elizabeth, the wonder of the world,
Over whose throne the enemies of God
Have thundered erst their vain, successless braves.
O ten-times-treble happy men that fight

Under the cross of Christ and England's Queen,
And follow such as Drake and Norris are!
All honours do this cause accompany;
All glory on these endless honours waits:
These honours and this glory shall he send
Whose honours and whose glory you defend.

My Fishful Pond is my Delight.

RICHARD CAREW (1555–1620), born at East Antony, was the author of the *Survey of Cornwall*, from which the following quaint lines, descriptive of a fish-pond which he had made, are taken.

WAYT not at the lawyer's gates—
    Ne shoulder clymers down the stayres;
I vaunt not manhood by debates,
    I envy not the miser's feares:
But meane in state, and calm in sprite,
My fishfull pond is my delight.

Where equall distant Iland viewes
    His forced banks, and otters' cage:
Where salt and fresh the poole renues,
    As spring and drowth encrease or swage:
Where boat presents his service prest,
And net becomes the fishes nest;

There sucking millet, swallowing basse,
    Side-walking crab, wry-mouthed flooke,

And slip-fist eele, as evenings passe,
    For safe bayt at due place doe looke:
Bold to approche, quick to espy,
Greedy to catch, ready to fly.

In heat the top, in cold the deepe;
    In spring the mouth, the mids in neap:
With changelesse change by shoales they keepe,
    Fat, fruitfull, ready, but not cheap:
Thus meane in state, and calm in sprite,
My fishfull pond is my delight.

The Well of St. Keyne.

CAREW, in his *Survey* aforesaid. The trees are gone, and the well is dry; but the tradition remains.

IN name, in shape, in quality,
    This well is very quaint;
The name to lot of Kayne befell,
    No over-holy saint.
The shape—four trees of divers kinde,
    Withy, oke, elme, and ash,
Make with their roots an arched roofe,
    Whose floore this spring doth wash.
The quality—that man or wife,
    Whose chance or choice attaines,
First of this sacred streame to drinke,
    Thereby the mastry gaines.

The Combat of Corinæus and Goemagot.

MICHAEL DRAYTON (1563-1631) was born in Warwickshire. His *Polyolbion* contains many references to Devon and Cornwall. The extract below describes the legendary fight between Corinæus and Goemagot (the Gog and Magog of London Guildhall) on the Plymouth Hoe.

WHEN, forraging this Ile, long promis'd them before,
    Amongst the ragged Cleeues those monstrous Giants sought:
Who (of their dreadful kind) t' appall the Troians, brought
Great *Gogmagog*, an Oake that by the roots could teare:
    So mightie were (that time) the men who liued there:
But, for the vse of Armes he did not vnderstand
(Except some rock or tree, that comming next to hand
Hee raz'd out of the earth to execute his rage),
He challenge makes for strength, and offereth there his gage,
Which *Corin* taketh vp, to answer by and by,
Vpon this sonne of Earth his vtmost power to try.
All doubtful to which part the victorie would goe,
Vpon that loftie place at *Plinmouth*, call'd the *Hoe*,
Those mightie Wrastlers met; with many an irefull looke
Who threatned, as the one hold of the other tooke :

But, grapled, glowing fire shines in their sparkling eyes.
And, whilst at length of arme one from the other lyes,
Their lusty sinewes swell like cables, as they striue:
Their feet such trampling make, as though they forc't to driue
A thunder out of earth; which stagger'd with the weight:
Thus, eithers vtmost force vrg'd to the greatest height.
Whilst one vpon his hip the other seekes to lift,
And th' adverse (by a turne) doth from his cunning shift,
Their short-fetcht troubled breath a hollow noise doth make,
Like bellowes of a Forge. Then *Corin* vp doth take
The Giant twixt the grayns; and voyding of his hould
(Before his combrous feet he well recouer could)
Pitcht head-long from the hill; as when a man doth throw
An Axtree, that with sleight deliuerd from the toe
Rootes vp the yeelding earth: so that his violent fall,
Strooke *Neptune* with such strength, as shouldred him withall;
That where the monstrous waues like Mountaines late did stand,
They leap't out of the place, and left the bared sand
To gaze vpon wide heauen: so great a blowe it gaue.
For which, the conquering *Brute*, on *Corineus* braue
This horne of land bestow'd, and markt it with his name;
Of *Corin*, *Cornwall* call'd, to his immortall fame.

The Christian's Answer to the Epicure.

John Downe (1570-1631), born at Holsworthy.

EPICURE.

IME doth haste,
  Life as a shadow flies;
  Breath as a vapor soon doth waste,
And none returns that dies.
Come, let us banish woes,
  And live while life does last;
Crown we our heads with budding roses,
  And of each pleasure taste.
What, though precise fools do us blame,
  Shall we forego content?
Pleasure and substance; virtue, name,
  And life, will soon be spent.

CHRISTIAN.

Time shall cease,
  Archangel's trump shall sing;
Death shall its prisoners all release,
  And them to judgment bring.
Then shall these sinful joys
  To endless wailing turn,
And they that scorned virtue's choice
  In brimstone flames shall burn;
Then they that erst fond stoicks
  Shall wisdom's children prove,
When they among the saints esteemed
  Shall reign with Christ above.

Sir Francis Drake's Choice.

C. Fitz-Geoffry (1575-1636), born at Fowey, a clergyman, vicar of St. Dominick. The stanzas are from his *Life of Sir Francis Drake*.

LOOK how the industrious bee in fragrant May,
When Flora gilds the earth with golden flowers,
Inveloped in her sweet perfumed array,
Doth leave his honey-lined delicious bowers—
More richly wrought than princes' stately towers—
  Waving his silken wings amid the air,
  And to the verdant gardens makes repair.

First falls he on a branch of sugared thyme,
Then from the marygold he sucks the sweet,
And then the mint and then the rose doth climb,
Then on the budding rosemary doth light;
Till, with sweet treasure having charged his feet,
  Late in the evening home he turns again:
  Thus profit is the guerdon of his pain.

So in the May-tide of his summer age
Valour enmoved the mind of vent'rous Drake
To lay his life with winds and waves in gage,
And bold and hard adventures t' undertake—
Leaving his country for his country's sake;
  Loathing the life that cowardice doth stain,
  Prefering death if death might honour gain.

A Dirge.

This and the seven following extracts are from the dramatic works of JOHN FORD (1586-1640?), who was born at Ilsington, in Devon, and after spending the principal years of his life in London, returned to his native place, where he is believed to have died. In the *Time's Poets* there occurs the following couplet concerning him :

    Deep in a dump John Forde was alone got,
    With folded arms and melancholy hat.

GLORIES, pleasures, pomps, delights, and ease,
    Can but please
Our outward senses, when the mind
Is or untroubled or by peace refined.
Crowns may flourish and decay ;
Beauties shine, but fade away.
Youth may revel, yet it must
Lie down in a bed of dust.
Earthly honours flow and waste,
Time alone doth change and last.
Sorrows, mingled with contents, prepare
    Rest for care ;
Love only reigns in death ; though art
Can find no comfort for a broken heart.
              The Broken Heart.

VANITAS VANITATUM.

    Fools, desperate fools !
You are cheated, grossly cheated ; range, range on.
And roll about the world to gather moss,
The moss of honour, gay reports, gay clothes,

Gay wives, huge empty buildings, whose proud roofs
Shall with their pinnacles even reach the stars!
Ye work and work like blind moles, in the paths
That are bored through the crannies of the earth,
To charge your hungry souls with such full surfeits
As, being gorged once, make you lean with plenty;
And when you have skimmed the vomit of your riots,
You are fat in no felicity but folly:
Then your last sleeps seize on you; then the troops
Of worms crawl round, and feast, good cheer, rich cheer,
Dainty, delicious!

  MELEANDER, *The Lovers' Melancholy*, act ii. sc. 2.

MINUTES are numbered by the fall of sands,
As by an hour-glass; the span of time
Doth waste us to our graves, and we look on it:
An age of pleasures, revelled out, comes home
At last, and ends in sorrow; but the life,
Weary of riot, numbers every sand,
Wailing in sighs, until the last drop down;
So to conclude calamity in rest.

  ERODEA, *Ibid*, act iv. sc. 3.

ATHEISM.

DISPUTE no more on this; for know, young man,
These are no school points; nice philosophy
May tolerate unlikely arguments,
But heaven admits no jest: wits that presumed

A DIRGE.

On wit too much, by striving how to prove
There was no God, with foolish grounds of art,
Discovered first the nearest way to hell;
And filled the world with devilish atheism.
Such questions, youth, are fond: far better 'tis
To bless the sun than reason why it shines;
Yet He thou talk'st of is above the sun.
THE FRIAR, *'Tis Pity*, act i. sc. 1.

DESCRIPTION OF HELL.

     There is a place—
List, daughter! in a black and hollow vault,
Where day is never seen; there shines no sun,
But flaming horrors of consuming fires,
A lightless sulphur choaked with smoky fogs
Of an infected darkness: in this place
Dwell many thousand thousand sundry sorts
Of never dying deaths: there damned souls
Roar without pity; there are gluttons fed
With toads and adders; there is burning oil
Poured down the drunkard's throat; the usurer
Is forced to sup whole draughts of molten gold;
There is the murderer for ever stabbed,
Yet can he never die; there lies the wanton
On racks of burning steel, whilst in his soul
He feels the torment of his raging lust.
THE FRIAR, *Ibid*, act iii. sc. 4.

THE VOYAGE OF LIFE.

When a man has been an hundred years
Hard travelling o'er the tottering bridge of age,
He's not the thousandth part upon his way:
All life is but a wandering to find home;
When we are gone we're there. Happy were man,
Could here his voyage end; he should not then
Answer how well or ill he steered his soul
By heaven's or by hell's compass; how he put in
(Losing blest goodness' shore) at such a sin;
Nor how life's dear provision he has spent,
Nor how far he in's navigation went
Beyond commission: this were a fine reign
To do ill and not hear of it again;
Yet then were man more wretched than a beast;
For, sister, our dead pay is sure the best.

   Frank, *Witch of Edmonton*, act iv. sc. 2.

DEATH.

Death? pish! 'tis but a sound, a name of air;
A minute's storm, or not so much; to tumble
From bed to bed, be massacred alive
By some physicians, for a month or two
In hope of freedom from a fever's torments,
Might stagger manhood; here the pain is past
Ere sensibly 'tis felt. Be men of spirit.

Spurn coward passion! so illustrious mention
Shall blaze our names and style us kings o'er death.
WARBECK, *Perkin Warbeck*, act i. sc. 3.

LIFE? ah, no life, but soon extinguished tapers!
Tapers? no tapers, but a burnt-out light!
Light? ah, no light, but exhalations vapours!
Vapours? no vapours, but ill-blinded sight!
Sight? ah, no sight, but hell's eternal night!
  A night? no night, but picture of an elf!
  An elf? no elf, but very death itself!
Fame's Memorial.

Sir Francis Drake; or, Eighty-eight.

HARL. MS., 791, fol. 59.

IN eyghtye-eyght, ere I was borne,
  As I can well remember,
In August was a fleet prepared,
  The moneth before September.

Spayne, with Biscayne, Portugall,
  Toledo, and Granado,
All these did meet, and made a fleet,
  And called it the Armado.

When they had gott provision,
  As mustard, pease, and bacon;
Some say two shipps were full of whipps,
  But I thinke they were mistaken.

There was a litle man of Spaine
  That shott well in a gunn-a—
Don Pedro bright, as good a knight
  As the knight of the sunn-a.

King Phillip made him Admiral,
  And charged him not to stay-a—
But to destroy both man and boy,
  And then to runn away-a.

The King of Spayne did freet amayne,
  And to doe yet more harme-a,
He sent along to make him strong
  The famous Prince of Parma.

When they had sayl'd along the seas,
  And anchoréd uppon Dover,
Our Englishmen did board them then,
  And cast the Spaniards over.

Oure Queene was then att Tilbury;
  What could you more desire-a?
For whose sweete sake Sir Francis Drake
  Did sett them all on fyre-a.

But let them look about themselfes;
  For if they come again-a,
They shall be served with that same sauce
  As they were, I know when-a.

Sir Francis Drake and Queen Elizabeth.

From *Wit and Drollery*, 1656.

SIR FRANCIS, Sir Francis, Sir Francis his son,
Sir Robert and eke Sir William did come;
And eke the good Erle of Southampton
Marcht on his way most gallantly;
And then the Queen began to speeke:
You are welcome home, Sir Francis Drake;
Then came my Lord Chamberlain, and with his white staffe,
And all the people began for to laugh.

THE QUEEN'S SPEECH.

GALLANTS all of British blood,
Why do not ye saile on th' ocean flood?
I protest ye are not all worth a philberd,
Compared with Sir Humphry Gilberd.

THE QUEEN'S REASON.

For he walkt forth in a rainy day;
To the New-found-land he took his way
With many a gallant fresh and green:
He never came home again. God bless the Queen.

Disdain Returned.

THOMAS CAREW (1589-1639) came of a Devonshire family, though born in Gloucestershire. His poems were much admired by his contemporaries.

HE that loves a rosy cheek,
   Or a coral lip admires,
   Or from star-like eyes doth seek
Fuel to maintain his fires :
As old Time makes these decay,
So his flames must waste away.

But a smooth and steadfast mind,
   Gentle thoughts, and calm desires ;
Hearts with equal love combined ;
   Kindle never dying fires :
Where these are not, I despise
Lovely cheeks, or lips, or eyes.

No tears, Celia, now shall win
   My resolved heart to return ;
I have searched thy soul within,
   And find nought but pride and scorn.
I have learnt thy arts, and now
Can disdain as much as thou.

Some power in my revenge convey
That love to her I cast away.

Lydford Law.

WILLIAM BROWNE (1590-1645) was born at Tavistock, and, like other Western poets of note, is far too little known. His chief work is entitled *Britannia's Pastorals*, the best edition of which is that of Mr. Hazlitt. "Lydford Law" is remarkable for its humour, and the fact that portions have become proverbial. Lydford Castle was the old Stannary Prison, and quite deserved the character given to it. The date of this piece is probably 1644.

I OFT had heard of Lydford law,
How in the morn they hang and draw,
    And sit in judgment after.
At first I wondered at it much,
And now I find their reason such,
    That it deserves no laughter.

They have a castle on a hill;
I took it for some old wind-mill,
    The vanes blown off by weather.
Than lie therein one night, 'tis guessed,
'Twere better to be stoned, or pressed,
    Or hanged—now choose you whether!

Two men less room within this cave
Than five mice in a lantern have:
    The keepers, too, are sly ones:
If any could devise by art
To get it up into a cart,
    'Twere fit to carry lions.

When I beheld it, Lord! thought I,
What justice and what clemency
   Hath Lydford Castle's high hall!
I know none gladly there would stay,
But rather hang out of the way
   Than tarry for a trial.

The Prince a hundred pounds hath sent
To mend the leads and planchings rent
   Within this living tomb;
Some forty-five pounds more had paid
The debts of all that shall be laid
   There till the day of doom.

One lies there for a seam of malt,
Another for two pecks of salt,
   Two sureties for a noble.
If this be true, or else false news,
You may go ask of Master Crews,
   John Vaughan, or John Doble.*

Near to the men that lie in lurch,
There is a bridge, there is a church,
   Seven ashes, and an oak;
Three houses standing and ten down:
They say the parson hath a gown,
   But I saw ne'er a cloak:

---

* Crews was the steward, and the others attorneys.

Whereby you may consider well
That plain simplicity doth dwell
   At Lydford without bravery;
And in that town both young and grave
Do love the naked truth, and have,
   No clokes to hide their knavery.

This town's enclosed with desert moors,
But where no bear nor lion roars,
   And nought can live but hogs:
For all o'erturned by Noah's flood,
Of fourscore miles scarce one foot's good,
   The hills are wholly bogs.

And near hereto's the Gubbins'* cave—
A people that no knowledge have
   Of law, of God, or men:
Whom Cæsar never yet subdued;
Who've lawless lived; of manners rude;
   All savage in their den.

By whom, if any pass that way,
He dares not the least time to stay,
   For presently they howl;
Upon which signal they do muster
Their naked forces in a cluster,
   Led forth by Roger Rowle.

* These people were a kind of Devonshire banditti. They are mentioned by Fuller.

The people all within this clime
Are frozen in the winter time,
   Or drowned with snow or rain;
And when the summer is begun
They lie like silk-worms in the sun,
   And come to life again.

'Twas told me, 'In King Cæsar's time
The town was built of stone and lime,'
   But sure the walls are clay;
For they are fallen for aught I see,
And since the houses were got free—
   The town is run away.

O Cæsar! if thou there didst reign,
While one house stands, come there again;
   Come quickly, while there's one;
For if thou stayest one little fit,
But five years more, they may commit
   The whole town to a prison.

To see it thus, much grieved was I;
The proverb saith 'sorrows be dry,'
   So was I at the matter:
When by good luck, I know not how,
There thither came a strange stray cow,
   And we had milk and water.

Sure I believe it then did rain
A cow or two from Charles his wain;
   For none alive did see

Such kind of creatures there before,
Nor shall from hence for evermore
　　Save prisoners, geese, and we.

To nine good stomachs with our whigg,
At last we got a tithen pig,
　　This diet was our bounds;
And this was just as if 'twere known
A pound of butter had been thrown
　　Among a pack of hounds.

One glass of drink I got by chance,
'Twas claret when I was in France,
　　But now from it nought wider.
I think a man might make as good
With green crabs boiled with Brazil wood,
　　And half-a-pint of cider.

I kissed the mayor's hand of the town,
Who, though he wears no scarlet gown,
　　Honours the rose and thistle.
A piece of coral to the mace,
Which there I saw to serve the place,
　　Would make a good child's whistle.

At six o'clock I came away,
And prayed for those that were to stay
　　Within a place so arrant:
Wild and ope to winds that roar,
By God's grace I'll come there no more,
　　Unless by some tin-warrant.

To Devon.

WILLIAM BROWNE.

HAIL, thou, my native soil! thou blessed plot,
Whose equal all the world affordeth not!
Show me who can so many crystal rills,
Such sweet clothed valleys, or aspiring hills;
Such wood, grand pastures, quarries, wealthy mines,
Such rocks in which the diamond fairly shines;
And if the earth can show the like again,
Yet will she fail in her sea-ruling men.
Time never can produce men to o'ertake
The fames of Grenville, Davies, Gilbert, Drake,
Or worthy Hawkins, or of thousands more,
That by their power made the Devonian shore
Mock the proud Tagus; for whose richest spoil
The boasting Spaniard left the Indian soil
Bankrupt of store, knowing it would quit cost
By winning this, though all the rest were lost.

Farewell to Deanbourne.

ROBERT HERRICK (1591-1674), though born in London, resided so many years at Dean Prior, in Devon, of which he was vicar, as to justify this quotation of some lines written when he was ejected from the vicarage (to which he was afterwards restored) in 1648.

DEANBOURNE, farewell; I never look to see
Deane, or thy warty incivility.
Thy rockie bottome that doth teare thy [streames,
And makes them frantick, e'en to all extreames;

To my content I never should behold,
Were thy streames silver, or thy rocks all gold.
Rockie thou art, and rockie we discover
Thy men, and rockie are thy ways all over.
Of men of manners now and ever known
To be a *Rockie generation!*
A people currish; churlish as the seas;
And rude almost as rudest salvages:
With whom I did and may re-sojourne when
Rocks turn to Rivers, Rivers turn to Men.

Inscription

On a cup of silver given by Sir Bevis Bulmer to the City of London in 1593, made out of silver raised at Coombe Martin.

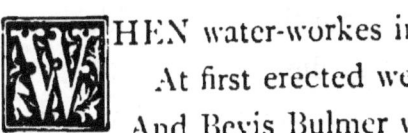HEN water-workes in Broaken Wharfe
    At first erected were,
And Bevis Bulmer with his art
    The waters 'gan to reare,
Disperced I in earth dyd lye,
    Since all beginninge olde,
In place called Comb, where Martin longe
    Had hid me in his molde.
I did no service in the earth,
    But no man set me free
Till Bulmer by his skill and charge
    Did frame me this to be.

Sir Francis Drake.

THE following lines are inscribed beneath the original portrait of Sir Francis Drake, in the possession of the Corporation of Plymouth.

SIR DRAKE, whom well the world's end knew
    Which thou didst compass round,
And whom both poles of heaven once saw,
    Which North and South doe bound.
The starrs above will make thee known
    If men here silent were :
The Sun himself cannot forget
    His fellow Traveller !

Great Drake, whose shippe about the world's wide waste
In three years did a golden girdle cast ;
Who with fresh streams refresht this towne that first,
Though kist with waters, yet did pine with thirst.
Who, both a pilote and a magistrate,
Steered in his turn the Shippe of Plymouth's State ;
This little table shewes his face, whose worth,
The world's wide table hardly can set forth.

Plymouth in 1625.

WILLIAM STRODE (1598-1644) was one of the Strodes of Newnham, near Plympton, another member of which family was one of the famous "five members" whom Charles I. went to the House of Commons to seize. The male line failed in 1874 by the death of Major Strode, its last representative. This poem is the earliest example of the Devonshire dialect on record. The visit of the King alluded to was in 1625.

THOU n'ere woot riddle, neighbour John,
   Where ich of late have bin-a ;
Why ich have bin to Plimoth, man,
   The like was yet n'ere zeene-a :
Zich streets, zich men, zich hugeous zeas,
   Zich things and guns there rumbling,
Thyzelf, like me, wood'st blesse to zee
   Zich bomination grumbling.

The streets be pight of shingle-stone,
   Doe glissen like the sky-a,
The zhops ston ope and all ye yeere long
   I 'se think a faire there bee-a-.
And many a gallant here goeth
   I' goold, that zaw the King-a- ;
The King zome zweare himself was there,
   A man or zome zich thing-a-.

Thou voole, that never water zaw'st,
   But think-a in the Moor-a-,

To zee the zea, wood'st be a'gast,
    It doth zoo rage and roar-a :
It tast's zoo zalt thy tonge wood thinke
    The vire were in ye water ;
And, tis zoo wide, noe lond is spide,
    Look nere zoo long there-ater.

The water from the element
    Noe man can zee chi-vore ;
'Twas zoo low, yet all consent
    'Twas higher than the Moor.
'Tis strange how looking down a cliffe,
    Men do looke upward rather,
If there mine eyne had not it zeene,
    'Chood scarce believe my vather.

Amidst the water wooden birds,
    And flying houses zwim-a- ;
All full of things as ich ha' heard,
    And goods up to ye brim-a- ;
They goe unto another world,
    Desiring to conquier-a-,
Vor wch those guns, voule develish ones,
    Do dunder and spett vire-a-.

Good neighbor John, how var is this ?
    This place vor I will zee-a- ;
'Ch'ill moape no longer heere, that's flat,
    To watch a zheepe or zheene-a- ;

Though it zoo var as London bee,
Wch ten miles ich imagin,
'Ch 'll thither hye, for this place I
Do take in great induggin.

An Invocation.

ALEXANDER DANIEL (1599-1668), the son of Richard Daniel, of Truro, was born in the Low Countries, but settled at Lariggan, near Penzance. This invocation is prefixed to a large volume of poetry by him, which still remains in MS.

IF it may pleasing be in poesie
    To laud the Lord, then leave I humbly crave
To cast my mite into God's treasurie,
    It is even all the abilities I have;
'Tis all I have, and yet it is not mine;
It is the Lord's in what it is divine.

Give unto Cæsar what is Cæsar's due;
    It is the tribute of a loyal heart.
O grant, good God, some profit may ensue
    Hence to Thy church; then I have done my part.
If hence to Thine some good may yet redound,
Lord, let it not be buried in the ground.

God no respecter of men's persons is;
    The poor may praise His name as well as rich.
Grant, gracious Giver of all good, that this
    (If nothing else) at least incite may such
To whom Thou greatest gifts hast given, that they
More perfectly Thy praises may display.

Enkindle, Lord, my cold and slow desire;
   And not mine only, but revive in all
Th' almost extinguished spark of holy fyre!
   Let one cole from Thine heavenly altar fall,
And it the affections of Thy fold inflame,
To sing sweet anthems to Thy glorious name.

Lord, let not the last age be wholly lost,
   And drowned in senseless, dull securitie!
Save yet a remnant, Lord, although the most
   Are led away with foul impuritie!
Lest ev'n Thy chosen should of ill partake,
Shorten Thy coming, Lord, for Zion's sake!

Good meditations from God's Spirit flow—
   Each pious thought proceedeth from the Lord,
How are our hearts become so hardened now
   They are no more affected with God's word;
Seeing that as our bodies perish here,
Our soul's redemption daily draweth near?

If at Christ's coming in the flesh began
   His kingdom upon earth, what shall we say?
Since it's 'bove sixteen hundred years agone,
   Far off sure cannot be the judgment-day!
We may not think the Lord will long delay
His coming now! then be it all our care
Ourselves against His coming to prepare.

Oberon's Wardrobe.

This fanciful composition is from *Musarum Deliciæ*, a work which was the joint production of Sir JOHN MENNIS (1598-1670), born at Sandwich, controller of the navy for Charles I. and II.; and Dr. JAMES SMITH (1604-1667), reputed to be of Devonshire birth, canon and chanter of Exeter Cathedral.

WHEN the monthly horned queen
Grew jealous that the stars had seen
Her rising from Endymion's arms,
   In rage she throws her misty charms
   Into the bosom of the night,
   To dim their curious prying light.

Then did the dwarfish fairy elves
(Having first attired themselves)
Prepare to dress their Oberon King
In highest robes for revelling :
   In a cobweb shirt more thin
   Than ever spider since could spin ;
Bleached to the whiteness of the snow,
As the stormy winds did blow
It in the vast and freezing air ;
No shirt half so fine, so fair.

A rich waistcoat they did bring,
Made of the trout-fly's gilded wing.
   *   *   *   *

The outside of his doublet was
Made of the four-leaved true love grass.
  * * * *
On every seam there was a lace
Drawn by the unctuous snail's slow trace;
To it the finest silver thread,
Compared, did look like dull, pale lead.
Each button was a sparkling eye,
Ta'en from the speckled adder's fry,
Which in a gloomy night and dark
Twinkled like a fiery spark :
And for coolness, next his skin
'Twas with white poppy lined within.
  * * * *
A rich mantle he did wear,
Made of tinsel gossamer,
Bestarred over with a few
Diamond drops of morning dew.
His cap was all of ladies' love ;
So passing light that it did move
If any humming gnat or fly
But buzzed the air in passing by.
About it was a wreath of pearl
Dropped from the eyes of some poor girl,
Pinched because she had forgot
To leave fair water in the pot ;
And for feather he did wear
Old Nisus' fatal purple hair.

The sword they girded on his thigh
Was smallest blade of finest rye.
A pair of buskins they did bring
Of the cow-lady's* coral wing,
Powdered o'er with spots of jet,
And lined with purple-violet.
His belt was made of myrtle leaves,
Plaited in small, curious threaves,
Beset with amber cowslip studs,
And fringed about with daisy buds;
In which his bugle-horn was hung,
Made of the babbling Echo's tongue.

Constant Love.

SIDNEY GODOLPHIN (1609-1643) was a member of the ancient Cornish family of that name, now represented by the Duke of Leeds. He took the King's side in the Civil War, and was slain, bravely fighting, at Chagford. There is an old couplet referring to the chief cavalier leaders of the West, which runs:

> The four wheels of Charles's wain—
> Grenville, Godolphin, Trevanion, Slanning—slain.

'TIS affection but dissembled,
  Or dissembled liberty,
To pretend thy passion changed
  With changes of thy mistress' eye—
    Following her inconstancy.

* The lady-bird.

Hopes which do from favour flourish
    May perhaps as soon expire
As the cause which did them nourish,
    And disdained they may retire;
    But love is another fire.

For if beauty cause thy passion;
    If a fair, resistless eye
Melt thee with its soft expression—
    Then thy hopes will never die;
    Nor be cured by cruelty.

'Tis not scorn that can remove thee;
    For thou either wilt not see
Such loved beauty not to love thee,
    Or will else consent that she
    Judge not as she ought of thee.

Thus thou either canst not sever
    Hope from what appears so fair,
Or unhappier thou canst never
    Find contentment in despair—
    Nor make love a trifling care.

There are seen but few retiring
    Steps in all the paths of love,
Made by such who in aspiring
    Meeting scorn their hearts remove;
    Yet e'en these ne'er change their love.

Verses

AFFIXED to the wall of the prison at the Plymouth Guildhall, where the writer was detained a month before being sent into captivity at Drake's Island, Plymouth Sound. ABRAHAM CHEARE, who wrote them, was the first recorded pastor of the Baptist Church in Plymouth, and died in his island confinement, 1668. He wrote a volume of religious poetry.

IGH four years since, sent out from hence
    To Exon gaol was I;
But special grace in three months' space
    Wrought out my liberty.
Till Bartholomew in sixty-two
    That freedom did remain;
Then without bail to Exon gaol
    I hurried was again.

Where having layn, as doe the slain,
    'Mong dead men wholly free;
Full three years' space, my native place
    By leave I came to see;
And thought not then, I here again
    A month's restraint should find,
Since to my den cast out from men
    I'm during life designed.

But since my lines the Lord assigns
    In such a lot to be,
I kiss the rod, confess my God
    Deals faithfully with me.

My charged crime in His due time
He fully will decide:
And until then, forgiving men,
In peace with Him I bide.

Song.

Rev. Henry Killigrew, Master of the Savoy (1613-1700), born at Hanworth, a member of the ancient Cornish family of Killigrew, of Arwenack. The song is from his tragedy of *The Conspiracy*, where it is introduced as sung in a dream to the rightful heir to the throne, who is kept from his inheritance. Henry Killigrew's daughter, Anne (1660-1685), maid of honour to the Duchess of York, also wrote poetry, which was published after her death; and other members of the family must likewise be numbered among Western poets.

HILE Morpheus thus does gently lay
His powerful charge upon each part,
Making the spirits ev'n obey
The silver charms of his dull art;

I, thy good angel, from thy side—
As smoke doth from the altar rise,
Making no noise as it doth glide—
Will leave thee in this soft surprise;

And from the clouds will fetch thee down
A holy vision to express
Thy right unto an earthly crown;
No power can make this kingdom less.

But gently, gently, lest I bring
   A start in sleep by sudden flight,
Playing aloof and hovering,
   Till I am lost unto the sight.

This is a motion still and soft;
   So free from noise and cry,
That Jove himself, who hears a thought,
   Knows not when we pass by.

The Trimmer.

Tom D'Urfey (1628-1723), born at Exeter, of French descent, a voluminous writer of songs, ballads, political and other verses, for the most part of a casual and ephemeral character. The picture drawn in the following stanzas, though bearing the stamp of the time when it was written, is not without satiric touches of present application. It is to the favourite old tune, "Which nobody can deny," the chorus being repeated after each stanza.

PRAY lend me your ear, if you've any to spare,
   You that love Commonwealth as you hate
      common prayer,
Which can in a breath pray, dissemble, and swear—
      Which nobody can deny, deny,
      Which nobody can deny.

I'm first on the wrong side, and then on the right;
To-day I'm a Jack,* and to-morrow a mite;
I for either king pray, but for neither dare fight.

      * Jacobite.

Sometimes I'm a rebel, sometimes I'm a saint;
Sometimes I can preach, and at other times can't;
There is nothing but grace, thank God, that I want

Of our gracious King William I am a great lover,
Yet I side with a party that prays for another;
I'd drink the King's health, take it one way or t'other.

Precisely I creep like a snail to the meeting,
Where sighing I sit, and such sorrowful greeting
Makes me hate a long prayer and two hours' prating.

And then I sing psalms as if never weary;
Yet I must confess when I'm frolic and merry
More music I find in *A Boat to the Ferry;*

I can pledge every health my companions drink round;
I can say *heaven bless*, or the *devil confound;*
I can hold with the hare and run with the hound.

I can pray for a bishop, and curse an archdeacon;
I can seem very sorry that Charleroi's taken;
I can say anything to save my own bacon.

Sometimes for a good Commonwealth I am wishing,
O Oliver! Oliver! give us thy blessing!
For in troubled waters now I love fishing;

The times are so ticklish I vow and profess,
I know not which party or cause to embrace—
I'll side with those, be sure, that are least in distress.

With the Jacks I rejoice that Savoy's* defeated;
With the Whigs I seem pleased he so bravely retreated;
Friends and foes are by me both equally treated:

Each party, you see, is thus full of great hope;
There are some for the Devil, and some for the Pope;
And I am for anything—but for a rope.

The Lord Protector Cromwell.

Thomas Sprat (1636-1713), born at Tallaton, Devon, became Bishop of Rochester. The quotation is from his warmly eulogistic ode to the memory of Cromwell.

WILL thou command'st, that azure chain of waves
   Which nature round about us sent,
     Made us to every pirate slaves,
  Was rather burden than an ornament;
  Those fields of sea that washed our shores
Were ploughed and reaped by other hands than ours:
   To us the liquid mass
    Which doth about us run,
    As it is to the sun,
   Only a bed to sleep on was;
And not as now, a powerful throne
To shake and sway the world thereon.

      * The Duke of Marsiglia.

Our princes in their hand a globe did show,
   But not a perfect one—
 Composed of earth and waters too.
 But thy commands the floods obeyed;
   Thou all the wilderness of water swayed;
 Thou didst not only wed the sea—
 Not make her equal, but a slave to thee;
 Neptune himself did bear thy yoke,
   Stooped and trembled at ev'ry stroke;
    He that ruled all the main
    Acknowledged thee his sovereign:
 And now the conquered sea doth pay
 More tribute to thy Thames than that unto the sea.

   England till thou didst come
    Confined her valour home;
   Then our own rocks did stand
   Bounds to our fame as well as land,
    And were to us as well
    As to our enemies unpassable:
   We were ashamed at what we read,
   And blushed at what our fathers did;
 Because we came so far behind the dead.
 The British lion hung his mane and drooped;
   To slavery and burthen stopped;
    With a degenerate sleep and fear
 Lay in his den, and languished there;

    At whose least voice before
A trembling echo ran through every shore,
    And shook the world at every roar.
Thou his subdued courage didst restore,
    Sharpened his claws, and from his eyes
Madest the same dreadful lightnings rise;
Madest him again affright the neighbouring floods,
His mighty thunder sound through all the woods:
    Thou hast our military fame redeemed,
        Which was lost or clouded seemed.
    Nay, more, heaven did by thee bestow
On us at once an iron age, and happy too.

    Though Fortune did hang on thy sword,
        And did obey thy mighty word;
        Though Fortune for thy side and thee
        Forgot her loved inconstancy:
Amidst thy arms and trophies thou
Wert valiant and gentle too;
Woundedst thyself when thou didst kill thy foe.
    Like steel, when it much work has past—
    That which was rough does shine at last—
    Thy arms by being oftener used did smoother grow.
Nor did thy battles make thee proud or high;
    Thy conquest raised the State, not thee.
    Thou overcam'st thyself in every victory—
    As when the sun on a directer line
        Upon a polished golden shield doth shine,

The shield reflects unto the sun again his light:
So when the heaven smiled on thee in fight;
  When thy propitious God hath lent
  Success and victory to thy tent;
To heaven again the victory was sent.
Thou fought'st not to be high or great,
  Nor for a sceptre nor a crown,
  Or ermine, purple, or the throne;
    But as the vestal heat
  Thy fire was kindled from above alone:
  Religion putting on thy shield
  Brought these victorious to the field.
Thy arms like those which ancient heroes wore
  Were given by the God thou didst adore:
  And all the swords thy armies had
  Were on an heavenly anvil made;
Not interest, or any weak desire
Of rule or empire, did thy mind inspire:
  Thy valour, like the holy fire
  Which did before the Persian armies go,
Lived in the camp, and yet was sacred too:
  Thy mighty sword anticipates
What was designed by heaven and those blest feats,
And makes the church triumphant here below.

Sir Bevill Grenville.

THE following epitaph to the memory of Sir Bevill Grenville, killed at Lansdown, 1643, was written by MARTIN LLEWELLYN. The ancestor referred to is the great Sir Richard Grenville.

THUS slain thy valiant ancestor did lye,
When his one bark a navy did defy;
When now encompassed round the victor stood,
And bathed his pinnace in his conquering blood,
Till, all his purple current dried and spent,
He fell, and made the waves his monument.
Where shall the next famed Grenville's ashes stand—
Thy grandsire fills the seas, and thou the land?

On Sir John Eliot.

JOHN POLWHELE (died 1672), one of the ancient Cornish family of Polwhele of Polwhele. Sir John Eliot was one of the ancestors of the Earl of St. Germans, and one of the chief patriots of the time of Charles I., dying in prison in the Tower.

HEER a musitian lyes whose well-tuned tongue
Was great Apollo's harpe, so sweetly strunge
That every cadence was an harmonye.
Noe crotchets in his musicke! onlye hee
Charmed the attentive burgesses alonge,
Ledde by the eares to listen to his songe.

*   *   *   *   *

For innocence, sad widdowes' orphans' teares
(The dumbe petitioners of unfeigned feares),
How smoothly could thine eloquence alone
Create a helpinge pittie where was none.

To Chloris.

JOHN BULTEEL. The family of Bulteel is of French origin, and has long been settled in Devonshire.

HLORIS, 'twill be for either's rest
Truly to know each other's breast;
I'll make the obscurest part of mine
Transparent, as I would have thine:
   If you will deal but so with me,
   We soon shall part, or soon agree.

Know then though you were twice as fair,
If it could be, as now you are,
And though the graces of your mind
With a resembling lustre shined;
   Yet if you loved me not, you 'd see,
   I'd value that as you do me.

Though I a thousand times had sworn
My passion should transcend your scorn,
And that your bright, triumphant eyes
Create a flame that never dies;
   Yet if to me you proved untrue,
   These oaths should prove as false to you.

If love I vowed to pay for hate,
'Twas, I confess, a mere deceit;
Or that my flame should deathless prove,
'Twas but to render so your love;

I bragged as cowards use to do
Of dangers they'll ne'er run into.

And now my tenets I have showed,
If you think them too great a load;
T' attempt your charge were but in vain,
The conquest not being worth the pain:
　With them I'll other nymphs subdue;
'Tis too much to lose time and you.

Hymnus Vespertinus.

HENRY GRENFIELD, born at Truro, Master of Truro Grammar School, 1685-1693.

THRICE blest, my God and King,
　　　The only spring
Of every good and perfect thing.

Thou hast preserved my ways;
　　　Accept my praise:
This and all other my past days.

And now the shades come on:
　　　O living Sun,
Go not out of my horizon!

Stream forth thy glorious light,
　　　That I by night
May count my past day's sins aright.

But how shall I recall
　　　These errors all,
Which under numbers will not fall?

Oh, hide them in that night
　　　Which from our sight
Did take and hide the world's great light!

To thy all-piercing sight
　　　My darkest night
Is clearer than to us noon-light.

Oh, let this thought me bring
　　　To keep within,
My heart and hand from secret sin!

When I my clay undress,
　　　Do thou me bless
From rags of all unrighteousness.

Who knows where I may have
　　　My bed for grave?
Oh, then, receive my soul, and save!

Great Watch, on whom no sleep
　　　Doth ever creep,
In grateful rest I pray me keep—

From all malignant things
　　　Which darkness brings—
Under the shadow of thy wings;

Dart forth thy healthful beams,
        Dispel those steams
Which cause or cherish hurtful dreams.

Pitch round me angels' tent:
        And from thee sent,
Let them blest visions represent:

As on thy Jacob's night—
        A ladder bright—
Thee on the top, my shield and light;

Whilst they to thee ascend,
        And from thee bend
By turns thy jewels to defend.

So shall I, in thy arms,
        Circled from harms,
Be lulled to bliss with sweetest charms.

Whilst gently from above
        Thy favours prove
My safeguard and my bed of love.

When I awake, move me
        To sing of thee,
And meditate on thy mercy.

And with the morning's wings,
        As light begins,
To flie to thee, great King of kings.

The Visit.

NICHOLAS ROWE (1673-1718) was a member of a Devonshire family.

IT and beauty, t'other day,
Chanced to take me in their way;
And, to make the favour greater,
Brought the Graces and good nature.
Conversation care beguiling,
Joy in dimples ever smiling—
All the pleasures here below
Men can ask or gods bestow—
A jolly train, believe me! No;
There were but two—Lepell and How.*

The Visiting Lady.

R. LUCK, sometime master of Barnstaple Grammar School; from a Miscellany, published in 1736. Gay attended Luck's school, and derived some of his inspiration from him.

AYLOVE is drest, serene and sweet the air:
Roger must drive her, but she knows not where.
—"At Flippant's first, next Lovemore's set me down;
Last at Picquet's."—"They're all gone out of Town."

* Lady Harvey, and (subsequently) the poet's wife.

—"Then to St. James's I'll directly go;
To Lady Cantly I a visit owe."
—"Yours of last Tuesday she has not returned:
Ladies who don't punctilios keep are scorned.
Your debt to Lady Constance would you pay?"
"Hideous, she'll neither scandal talk, nor play."
—"Or Townley?"—"No, her Sir's an ill-bred fool—
Quadrille and visits are his ridicule.
Then she's a prude, and lives and talks by rule."
—"Madam, determine, or the night will come."
—"Then, Roger, drive me anywhere—but home."

Sweet William's Farewell to Black-eyed Susan.

JOHN GAY (1688-1732), born at Barnstaple. His Fables are well known, and his *Beggars' Opera* may still be said to keep the stage. His most popular production is, however, undoubtedly, that which follows:

ALL in the Downs the fleet was moored,
    The streamers waving in the wind,
When black-eyed Susan came on board.
    "Oh, where shall I my true love find?
Tell me, my jovial sailors, tell me true,
If my sweet William sails among the crew."

William, who high upon the yard
    Rocked with the billow to and fro,
Soon as her well-known voice he heard,
    He sighed, and cast his eyes below:

The cords slide swiftly through his glowing hands,
And (quick as lightning) on the deck he stands.

So the sweet lark, high-poised in air,
 Shuts close his pinions to his breast
(If chance his mate's shrill call he hear),
 And drops at once into her nest.
The noblest captain in the British fleet
Might envy William's lip those kisses sweet.

"O Susan, Susan, lovely dear,
 My vows shall ever true remain;
Let me kiss off that falling tear,
 We only part to meet again.
Change, as ye list, ye winds; my heart shall be
The faithful compass that still points to thee.

"Believe not what the landsmen say,
 Who tempt with doubts thy constant mind:
They 'll tell thee sailors when away,
 In every port a mistress find.
Yes, yes, believe them when they tell thee so,
For thou art present wheresoe'er I go.

"If to fair India's coast we sail,
 Thy eyes are seen in diamonds bright;
Thy breath is Afric's spicy gale;
 Thy skin is ivory, so white.
Thus every beauteous object that I view,
Wakes in my soul some charm of lovely Sue.

"Though battle call me from thy arms,
    Let not my pretty Susan mourn;
Though cannons roar, yet safe from harms,
    William shall to his dear return.
Love turns aside the balls that round me fly,
Lest precious tears should drop from Susan's eye."

The boatswain gave the dreadful word,
    The sails their swelling bosom spread;
No longer must she stay aboard:
    They kissed, she sighed, he hung his head;
Her lessening boat unwilling rows to land:
"Adieu!" she cries; and waves her lily hand.

Song.

REV. SAMUEL WESLEY, elder brother of John Wesley, born at Epworth, 1692. From a volume of poetry published while he was Master of Blundell School, Tiverton, 1736.

WHAT man in his wits had not rather be poor,
    Than for lucre his freedom to give?
Ever busy the means of his life to secure,
    And so ever neglecting to live.

Environed from morning to night in a crowd,
    Not a moment unbent or alone:
Constrained to be abject, though never so proud,
    And at every one's call but his own.

Still repining and longing for quiet each hour,
  Yet studiously flying it still;
With the means of enjoying his work in his power,
  But accurst with his wanting the will.

For a year must be past, or a day must be come,
  Before he has leisure to rest:
He must add to his store this or that pretty sum,
  And then will have time to be blest.

But his gains, more bewitching the more they increase,
  Only swell the desire of his eye;
Such a wretch let mine enemy live, if he please;
  Let not even mine enemy die.

Love.

GEORGE GRENVILLE, Lord Lansdowne (1667–1735), grandson of Sir Bevill Grenville, the last of the family who lived at their noble house at Stowe, long since destroyed. His collected works were published in 1734.

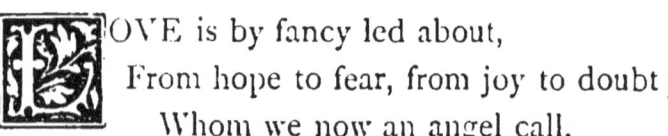OVE is by fancy led about,
  From hope to fear, from joy to doubt;
    Whom we now an angel call,
  Divinely graced in every feature,
  Straight's a deformed a perjured creature.
    Love and hate are fancy all;
    'Tis but as fancy shall present
    Objects of grief or of content,

That the Lover's blest or dies—
Visions of mighty pain or pleasure,
Imagined want, imagined treasure;
All in powerful fancy lies.

The Sea.

LYNE BRETT (1713-1741), born at Plymouth. He wrote a tragedy on the old story of the murder of "Page of Plymouth," by his wife and her lover, which still remains in MS., and numerous occasional pieces. The following was written on the Hoe.

GREAT GOD, though every work of thine
Proclaims its author all divine,
We in the ocean plainest see
The noblest attributes of thee.
When all is bright, when all serene,
When no rude winds disturb the main,
The shining prospect seems to prove
The mildness of the God I love.
But when the raging billows roar,
And foam and dash against the shore,
Then in the tempest does appear
The vengeance of the God I fear.
Methinks the wide-extended sea
Resembles thy immensity;
And, Lord, like thee, the vast profound,
Unfathomable too is found;

Like thee, the sea its blessings grants,
Though always giving, never wants,
Is ever full and still the same,
And nations only change its name.

The Apple-Dumplings and a King.

JOHN WOLCOTT, M.D. (1738–1819), born at Dodbrook, Devon, a voluminous satirical writer, who so frequently made George III. the theme of his rhymes, that, as he himself said, though the King was a good subject for him, he was a poor subject for the King. He wrote under the name of Peter Pindar.

ONCE on a time a monarch, tired with whooping,
    Whipping, and spurring,
      Happy in worrying
A poor, defenceless, harmless buck
(The horse and rider wet as muck),
From his high consequence and wisdom stooping,
    Entered through curiosity a cot,
  Where sat a poor old woman and her pot.

The wrinkled, blear-eyed, good old granny,
  In this same cot illumed by many a cranny,
Had finished apple-dumplings for her pot:
  In tempting row the naked dumplings lay,
  When, lo! the monarch, in his usual way,
Like lightning spoke, "What's this? what's this? what? what?"

Then, taking up a dumpling in his hand,
His eyes with admiration did expand,
    And oft did Majesty the dumpling grapple:
"'Tis monstrous, monstrous hard indeed (he cried);
What makes it, pray, so hard?" The dame replied,
    Low curtsying, "Please, your Majesty, the apple."

"Very astonishing indeed! Strange thing!
(Turning the dumpling round, rejoined the King)
    'Tis most extraordinary, then, all this is;
    It beats Pinetti's conjuring all to pieces;
Strange I should never of a dumpling dream!
But, Goody, tell me where, where, where's the seam?"

"Sir, there's no seam (quoth she); I never knew
That folks did apple-dumplings *sew*."
"No (cried the staring monarch with a grin),
How, how the devil got the apple in?"

On which the dame the curious scheme revealed,
By which the apple lay so sly concealed,
    Which made the Solomon of Britain start;
Who to the Palace with full speed repaired,
And Queen and Princesses so beauteous scared,
    All with the wonders of the dumpling art.
There did he labour one whole week to show
    The wisdom of an apple-dumpling maker;
And, lo! so deep was Majesty in dough,
    The Palace seemed the lodging of a baker.

Epigram

On a stone thrown at a very great man, but which missed him—
PETER PINDAR.

ALK no more of the lucky escape of the head
From a flint so unluckily thrown;
I think very different—with thousands indeed—
'Twas a lucky escape for the stone.

The Hare and the Bramble.

JAMES NORTHCOTE, R.A. (1746-1831), born at Plymouth, in his later years published two collections of fables. "The Hare and the Bramble" is among them.

 HARE, closely pursued, thought it prudent and meet
To a bramble for refuge awhile to retreat.
He entered the covert; but, entering, found
That briars and thorns did on all sides abound;
And that though he was safe, yet he never could stir,
But his sides they would wound, or would tear off his fur.
He shrugged up his shoulders, but would not complain:
"To repine at small evils," quoth puss, "is in vain;
That no bliss can be perfect I very well know,
But from the same source good and evil both flow;
And full sorely my skin though these briars may rend,
Yet they keep off the dogs, and my life will defend."
For the sake of the good then let evil be borne;
For each sweet has its bitter, each bramble its thorn.

Descriptions of Devonshire Scenery.

Rev. John Bidlake, D.D. (1751–1814), a native of Plymouth, became master of the Grammar School in that town, and held the position of Bampton lecturer in 1811. The quotations are from his *Year*, published in 1813.

HOW grateful now to trace the devious course
Of some wild pastoral stream, that changes oft
Its varied lapse, and ever as it winds
Enchantment follows, and new beauties rise.
Such thou, delightful Devon, hast to boast,
And such Cornubia—wild, romantic, both.
'Mid mountains rude, 'mid shadowy winding vales
Where streams melodiously in murmurs talk,
Or hoarse cascades to dreary solitudes
And nodding crags and rugged dales resound,
While latent echoes swell the solemn roar:
Such, Dart, thy rapid stream! thine, silver Plym!
Wild Teign, or Tamar, whose far-sweeping flood
The sister counties laves!

* * * * * * *

Where Tamar ocean joins with wedded waves
Mount Edgcumbe lifts his tree-clad rocks on high.
There groves on groves ascend, of every hue
And every growth; the gloomy pine, the oak,
The melancholy cypress, and the fir,

And all whose ever-living verdure scorns
E'en winter's darkest frown. Sweet interchange!—
Deep shade and sunny lawn—where fallow deer
With spotted sides disport; now browse in herds
The fragrant turf, now rustling through the glade,
Climb the high summit. What a glorious scene!
See ocean's blue expanse! How lightly glide
Yon barks! How proudly on the subject waves
Britannia's navy rides, that waits the call
To future triumphs! See, what rocky shores!
What castled cliffs arise! what towns and docks!
What rural sights, with rivers sparkling clear,
While mountains in the distance blend with sky!

* * * * * *

How sweet to fly the fervours of the sun,
And trace thy lucid steps, romantic Plym,
Up to the secret source, whence, stealing first,
Thy coy wave ventures to the day's broad beam.
See, bosomed deep in woody glens, and dark,
The silent stream creeps unperceived along
Its pebbled bottom, by the steepy bank,
And many an aged tree with twisted roots
And rugged boughs o'erhung. Where Sheepstor lifts
His towering height, what troublous cataracts dash
Adown the lichened rocks! Again the tide,
Stealing through Meavy's ivy-rocked bridge,
Flows rippling o'er a clear, unquiet bed.

Meavy, where flourished once illustrious Drake,
Who, drawing from the Naiad's copious urn,
Taught the young stream to wind beside the hill,
High o'er the vale, while Plymouth's distant sons
Drank pure libations from the wandering lymph.
Hark, how the river roars! What waving woods
Outstretch their quivering foliage o'er the wave,
Now lost beneath, now glittering with the rays
Of sparkling light! See! now it meets yon rock
Precipitous, yon crag with beetling brow,
With ashlings thick bestrewn, fixed in the clefts,
The orphans of the wood. High o'er the vale
Thy forehead, Dewerstone, enwrapped in clouds,
Frowns dark, while boiling at thy craggy feet
A sister torrent foams down steeps immense,
Till both, united, claim the name of Plym,
And, mingled, flow through Bickleigh's beauteous vale.

* * * * * *

What various tints of mosses, green or brown,
Or lichen hoary, or refulgent robed,
The antique limbs of yonder oak adorn!
How clear the lucid crystal of the stream!
Below the willowy-fringed bank, what shoals
Blacken the watery waste, myriads minute!
And where the giddy eddy winds his foam
The trout, bedropp'd with scarlet, lurks concealed;
Swift-darting through the solemn, shadowed pool,

Frequent they turn their silver-scaled sides,
Where, black upon the surface, stillness sleeps.
Reflection, in her imitative glass,
Inverts the nodding bough, the hanging rock;
While green transparence, with deceitful ray,
Uplifts the pebbly bottom of the tide;
Yet now and then a sudden leap disturbs
The liquid mirror, trembling to the shore.
Thus ever devious winds the lucid stream,
Till Saltram's shades conclude its varying course;
And, picturing on the clear, reflective wave
The fairy prospect, with a placid smile
Yields to vex'd ocean all its liquid wealth,
And ends, like placid age, its wearied steps.

On a Wet Summer.

JOHN BAMPFYLDE (1754-1796), of the Devonshire family of that name.

LL ye who far from town in rural hall,
 Like me, were wont to dwell near pleasant field,
  Enjoying all the sunny day did yield—
With me the change lament, in irksome thrall,
By rains incessant held; for now no call
  From early swain invites my hand to wield
  The scythe. In parlour dim I sit concealed,
And mark the lessening sand from hour-glass fall;

Or 'neath my window view the wistful train
Of dripping poultry, whom the vine's broad leaves
  Shelter no more. Mute is the mournful plain;
  Silent the swallow sits beneath the thatch,
  And vacant hind hangs pensive o'er his hatch,
Counting the frequent drip from reeded eaves.

To Peter Pindar.

WILLIAM GIFFORD (1756-1826), born at Ashburton, editor of the *Quarterly Review*, and author of numerous critical and satirical works. As an example of his powers of invective, the following is quoted from his "Ode to Peter Pindar" (Dr. Wolcott).

LO, here the reptile! who from some dark cell,
  Where all his veins with native poison swell,
  Crawls forth a slimy toad, and spits and spews
The crude abortions of his loathsome muse
On all that genius, all that worth holds dear—
Unsullied rank, and piety sincere;
While idiot mirth the base defilement lauds,
And malice, with averted face, applauds.

Lo, here the brutal sot! who, drenched with gin,
Lashes his wither'd nerves to tasteless sin;
Squeals out (with oaths and blasphemies between)
The impious song, the tale, the jest obscene;
And careless views, amidst the barbarous roar,
His few grey hairs strew, one by one, the floor!

Lo, here the wrinkled profligate! who stands
On nature's verge, and from his leprous hands
Shakes tainted verse; who bids us, with the price
Of rancorous falsehoods, pander to his vice,
Give him to live the future as the past,
And in pollution wallow to the last!

Enough! yet, Peter, mark my parting lay:
See, thy last sands are fleeting fast away,
And, what should more thy sluggish soul appal,
Thy limbs shrink up—the writing on the wall!
Oh check, a moment check, the obstreperous din
Of guilty joy, and hear the voice within;
The small, still voice of conscience, hear it cry,
An atheist thou mayst live, but canst not die!

Give then, poor tinkling bellman of fourscore,
Give thy lewd rhymes, thy lewder converse o'er,
Thy envy, hate;—and whilst thou yet hast power
On other thoughts employ the unvalued hour,
Lest as from crazy eld's diseaseful bed
Thou lift'st, to spit at heaven, thy palsied head,
The blow arrive, and thou, reduced by fate
To change thy frenzy for despair too late,
Close thy dim eyes a moment in the tomb,
To wake for ever in the world to come,
Wake to meet him whose "ord'nance thou hast slaved,"
Whose mercy slighted, and whose justice braved.

For me—why shouldst thou with abortive toil
Waste the poor remnant of thy sputtering oil
In filth and falsehood? Ignorant and absurd!
Pause from thy pains, and take my closing word;
Thou canst not think, nor have I power to tell,
How much I scorn and loathe thee—so farewell!

Winter.

Richard Polwhele (1760-1838), of the Polwheles of Polwhele, vicar of Manaccan, author of the Histories of Devon and Cornwall, various Translations, and other works.

WHILE not a wing of insect being floats,
    And not a murmur moves the frozen air,
    Yon ice-clad sedge, with tremulous wave denotes,
Amid the leafless copse, that life is there.
And, lo! half seen, the Bird of russet breast
    And duskier pinion, that had cleft the skies
Of wild inhospitable climes in quest
    Of the warm spring, his plashy labour plies.
Feed on, poor bird, beneath the sheltering copse;
    And near thee may no wanton spaniel stray!
Or rising, when dim eve her curtain drops,
    Ah, may no net arrest thy darkling way!
But long unpent by frost o'erflow the rill,
And many an insect meet thy delving bill.

Love.

SAMUEL TAYLOR COLERIDGE (1772-1834), born at Ottery St. Mary, the greatest poet the West of England has produced. His *Ancient Mariner* is familiar wherever the English tongue is known.

LL thoughts, all passions, all delights,
  Whatever stirs this mortal frame,
All are but ministers of Love,
  And feed his sacred flame.

Oft in my waking dreams do I
  Live o'er again that happy hour,
When midway on the mount I lay
  Beside the ruined tower.

The moonshine stealing o'er the scene
  Had blended with the lights of eve;
And she was there, my hope, my joy,
  My own dear Genevieve.

She leaned against the armed man,
  The statue of the armed knight;
She stood and listened to my lay
  Amid the lingering light.

Few sorrows hath she of her own,
  My hope! my joy! my Genevieve!
She loves me best whene'er I sing
  The songs that make her grieve.

I played a soft and doleful air,
I sang an old and moving story—
An old, rude song that suited well
    That ruin wild and hoary.

She listened with a flitting blush,
With downcast eyes and modest grace;
For well she knew I could not choose
    But gaze upon her face.

I told her of the Knight that wore
Upon his shield a blazing brand,
And that for ten long years he wooed
    The Lady of the Land.

I told her how he pined; and, ah!
The deep, the low, the pleading tone
With which I sang another's love
    Interpreted my own.

She listened with a flitting blush,
With downcast eyes and modest grace;
And she forgave me, that I gazed
    Too fondly on her face.

But when I told the cruel scorn
That crazed that bold and lovely Knight,
And that he crossed the mountain woods,
    Nor rested day nor night;

That sometimes from the savage den,
And sometimes from the darksome shade,
And sometimes starting up at once
    In green and sunny glade,

There came and looked him in the face
An angel beautiful and bright,
And that he knew it was a Fiend,
    The miserable Knight!

And that, unkenning what he did,
He leaped amid a murderous band,
And saved from outrage worse than death
    The Lady of the Land;

And how she wept and clasped his knees,
And how she tended him in vain,
And ever strove to expiate
    The scorn that crazed his brain;

And that she nursed him in a cave,
And how his madness went away,
When on the yellow forest-leaves
    A dying man he lay;

His dying words—but when I reached
That tenderest strain of all the ditty
My faltering voice and pausing harp
    Disturbed her soul with pity!

LOVE.

All impulses of soul and sense
Had thrilled my guileless Genevieve;
The music and the doleful tale,
    The rich and balmy eve;

And hopes, and fears that kindle hope,
An undistinguishable throng,
And gentle wishes long subdued,
    Subdued and cherished long!

She wept with pity and delight,
She blushed with love and virgin shame,
And like the murmur of a dream
    I heard her breathe my name.

Her bosom heaved—she stepped aside—
As conscious of my look she stept—
Then suddenly with timorous eye
    She fled to me and wept.

She half inclosed me in her arms,
She pressed me with a meek embrace;
And bending back her head, looked up
    And gazed upon my face.

'Twas partly love and partly fear,
And partly 'twas a bashful art,
That I might rather feel than see
    The swelling of her heart.

I calmed her fears, and she was calm
And told her love with virgin pride;
And so I won my Genevieve,
My bright and beauteous Bride.

Dartmoor.

NICHOLAS T. CARRINGTON (1777-1830), born at Devonport, where he was for many years a schoolmaster — the first descriptive poet of the West, certainly since the days of Browne. The extracts are from his principal poem, *Dartmoor*.

DARTMOOR! thou wert to me, in childhood's
    hour,
A wild and wondrous region. Day by day
Arose upon my youthful eye thy belt
Of hills mysterious, shadowy, clasping all
The green and cheerful landscape sweetly spread
Around my home; and with a stern delight
I gazed on thee. How often on the speech
Of the half-savage peasant have I hung,
To hear of rock-crowned heights on which the cloud
For ever rests; and wilds stupendous, swept
By mightiest storms; of glen, and gorge, and cliff
Terrific, beetling o'er the stone-strewed vale;
And giant masses, by the midnight flash
Struck from the mountain's hissing brow, and hurled
Into the foaming torrent! And of forms

That rose amid the desert, rudely shaped
By Superstition's hands when time was young;
And of the dead, the warrior dead, who sleep
Beneath the hallowed cairn! My native fields,
Though peerless, ceased to please. The flowery vale,
The breezy hill, the river, and the wood—
Island, reef, headland, and the circling sea,
Associated by the sportful hand
Of Nature, in a thousand views diverse—
Or grand or lovely—to my roving eye
Displayed in vain their infinite of charms:
I thought on thy wild world—to me a world—
Mysterious Dartmoor, dimly seen, and prized
For being distant and untrod; and still—
Where'er I wandered—still my wayward eye
Rested on thee.

* * * * *

How strangely on yon silent slopes the rocks
Are piled, and as I musing stray they take
Successive form deceptive. Sun and shower,
And breeze and storm, and haply ancient throes
Of this our mother earth, have moulded them
To shapes of beauty and of grandeur—thus;
And Fancy, all creative, musters up
Apt semblances. Upon the very edge
Of yonder cliff seem frowning o'er the vale
Time-hallowed battlements, with rugged chasms
Fearfully yawning; and upon the brow

Of yonder dreary hill are towers sublime,
Rifted as by the lightning stroke, or struck
By war's resistless bolts. The mouldering arch—
The long withdrawing aisle—the shattered shrine—
The altar gray with age—the sainted niche—
The choir breeze-swept, where once the solemn hymn
Upswelled—the tottering column—pile on pile
Fantastic—the imagination shapes
Amid these wrecks enormous. But 'tis o'er—
The dream is o'er, and reason dissipates
The fair illusions. Yet in truth ye wear,
Rocks of the desert, forms that on the eye
In solemn and imposing grandeur rise!
And even now, though near, the mountain seems
Strewed with innumerous fragments as when Fate
Mysterious, in some unexpected hour,
Inexorably casts at one fell blow
Fenced cities into ruinous heaps. O'er all
The rude but many-coloured lichen creeps;
And on the airy summit of yon hill,
Clasping the Tor's majestic brow, is seen
The dark funereal ivy, cheerless plant!
Which Death and Desolation wreathe around
Their haggard brows for ever.

    *   *   *   *   *

Nor waving crops, nor leaf, nor flowers adorn
Thy sides, deserted Crockern. Over thee
The winds have ever held dominion; thou

Art still their heritage, and fierce they sweep
Thy solitary hill what time the storm
Howls o'er the shrinking Moor.   The scowling gales
This moment slumber, and a dreary calm
Prevails—the calm of Death; the listless eye
Turns from thy utter loneliness.   Yet Man
In days long flown, upon the mount's high crest,
Has braved the highland gale, and made the rocks
Re-echo with his voice.   Not always thus
Has hovered, Crockern, o'er thy leafless scalp
The silence and the solitude that now
Oppresses the crushed spirit; for I stand
Where once the fathers of the forest held
(An iron race) the parliament that gave
The forest law.   Ye legislators, nursed
In lap of modern luxury, revere
The venerable spot where, simply clad,
And breathing mountain breezes, sternly sat
The hardy mountain council.   O'er them bent
No other dome but that in which the cloud
Sails—the blue dome of Heaven.   The ivy hung
Its festoons round the Tor, and at the foot
Of that rude fabric, piled by Nature, bloomed
The heath-flower.
   * * * * *
     On the gray
And naked rock, perchance once Nature strewed
The generous soil profusely; but the wrongs

Of centuries have made thee what thou art—
A howling desert in the loveliest isle
That ever ocean laved. One aged wood
Alone survives—the solitary wreck
Of all those hardy foresters which erst
Adorned, defended thee, and cheered the eye
Of the old mountaineer.
      How heavily
That old wood sleeps in the sunshine; not a leaf
Is trembling, not a wing is seen to move
Within it; but below, a mountain stream,
Conflicting with the rocks, is ever heard
Cheering the drowsy moor. Thy guardian oaks,
My country, are thy boast—a giant race,
And undegenerate still; but of this grove,
This pigmy grove, not one has climbed the air
So emulously that its loftiest branch
May brush the traveller's brow. The twisted roots
Have clasped, in search of nourishment, the rocks,
And straggled wide, and pierced the stony soil,
In vain: denied maternal succour here,
A dwarfish race has risen. Round the boughs
Hoary and feeble, and around the trunks,
With grasp destructive, feeding on the life
That lingers yet, the ivy winds, and moss
Of growth enormous. E'en the dull, vile weed
Has fixed itself upon the very crown
Of many an ancient oak; and thus refused

By Nature kindly aid—dishonoured—old—
Dreary in aspect silently decays
The lonely Wood of Wistman.

   * * * * *

       Earth
Reposes in the sunset. Let me gaze
At the great vision ere it pass; for now
The day-god hovers o'er the Western hill,
And sheds his last fond ray. Farewell, farewell!
Who givest beauty to the cloud, and light,
Joy, music to the earth! And must yon tints
And shapes divine which thou hast formed decay—
The mountain, and the temple, and the tower
That float in yonder fields of air; the isles
Of all surpassing loveliness; and seas
Of glorious emerald that seem to flow
Around the gold-fringed reefs and rocks;—must all
Vanish with thee at the remorseless touch
Of the swift coming twilight?

   * * * * *

     The night her ancient reign
Holds o'er the silent earth.

To the Tavy.

EDWARD ATKINS BRAY (1778-1857), born at Tavistock, and many years vicar of that place. The old house at Crowndale, where Drake was born, to which reference is here made, is now removed. Mr. Bray's poems were published in two volumes by his widow.

FT, Tavy! as I roam thy banks beside,
    The straw-thatched roof with fondest gaze I view
Where far-famed Drake his infant breath first drew,
Spain's dread destroyer, and Britannia's pride.
In Heaven confiding as his only guide,
    O'er unknown seas he led his daring crew;
    First o'er the globe the liquid circle drew,
And crowned Britannia empress of the tide.
Oh may these walls to times unborn remain,
    And tell how Heaven all bounteous has decreed
That native worth, though lowly, may attain
    From deathless Fame a mortal's highest meed!
Thus the tall tree that shades the subject plain
    Once crouched beneath its sod, a viewless seed.

To Laura.

WILLIAM KENDALL, Exeter, 1793.   Imitated from Guarini.

WHY frowns my fair? The mighty bliss
    Was bought with equal smart:
I rudely stole a rapturous kiss,
    I paid thee, with my heart.

St. Michael's Mount.

SIR HUMPHRY DAVY (1779-1829), born at Penzance. From an early volume of poems, published ere his great chemical discoveries had won him fame.

MAJESTIC Michael rises—he whose brow
    Is crowned with castles, and whose rocky sides
    Are clad with dusky ivy; he whose base,
Beat by the storms of ages, stands unmoved
Amidst the wreck of things—the change of time.
That base, encircled by the azure waves,
Was once with verdure clad: the towering oaks
Here waved their branches green—the sacred oaks,
Whose awful shades among the Druids strayed
To cut the hallowed mistletoe, and hold
High converse with their gods.

The Land's End.

SIR HUMPHRY DAVY.

N the sea
The sunbeams tremble, and the purple light
Illumes the dark Bolerium, seat of storms.
High are his granite rocks; his frowning brow
Hangs o'er the smiling ocean. In his caves
The Atlantic breezes murmur; in his caves,
Where sleep the haggard spirits of the storm.
Wild, dreary are the frowning rocks around,
Encircled by the wave, where to the breeze
The haggard cormorant shrieks; and far beyond,
Where the great ocean mingles with the sky,
Are seen the cloud-like islands, grey in mist.

Dolly Pentreath's Epitaph.

DOLLY PENTREATH is said to have been the last who used the old Cornish tongue. This epitaph was written by a Mr. THOMSON, of Truro, who had taken an interest in the Cornish language. It was not placed upon Dolly's tombstone, though popularly thought to be. The claims of Dorothy Pentreath to have been the last who spoke the Cornish have been disputed of late; nor is it likely that she really knew more of it than some of her contemporaries.

OTH Doll Pentreath, cans ha deau;
Marow ha kledyz ed Paul pleu:
Na ed an Eglos gan pobell bras,
Bes ed Eglos-hay coth Dolly es.

Old Dolly Pentreath, one hundred aged and two,
Both born and in Paul parish buried too;
Not in the church with people great and high,
But in the churchyard doth old Dolly lie.

Song in Old Cornish.

THESE stanzas are quoted as examples of the ancient Cornish language from Pryce's *Archæologia Cornu-Britannica*, 1790. The song bears a strong likeness to the familiar one, "Where are you going, my pretty maid?"

"PELEA era why moaz, moz fettow teag,
 Gen agaz bedgeth gwin, ha agaz blew mellyn?"
"Mi a moaz than venton, sarra wheag
 Rag delkiow sevi gwra muzi teag."

"Pea ve moaz gen a why, moz fettow teag,
 Gen agaz bedgeth gwin, ha agaz blew mellyn?"
"Greah mena why, sarra wheag,
 Rag delkiow sevi gwra muzi teag."

"Pray, whither so trippingly, pretty fair maid,
 With your face rosy white, and your soft yellow hair?"
"Sweet sir, to the well in the summer wood shade;
 For strawberry leaves make the young maiden fair."

"Shall I go with you, pretty fair maid, to the wood,
 With your face rosy white, and your soft yellow hair?"
"Sweet sir, if you please, it will do my heart good;
 For strawberry leaves make the young maiden fair."

Cornish Nonsense Verses.

DAVIES GILBERT (1767-1839), born at St. Erth, P.R.S. The first set of verses is a collection of the names of places in Cornwall, arranged in alternate rhyme by Mr. Davies Gilbert to show the euphony of the ancient Cornish tongue.

ELANDRUKYA Cracka Cudna,
Truzemenhall Chun Crowzanwrah,
Bans Burnuhal Brane Bosfrancan,
Treeve Trewhidden Try Trembah.

Carn Kanidgiac Castle-Skudjiac,
Beagle Tuben Amalvear,
Amalebria Amalwhidden,
Skillewadden Trink Polpeor.

Pellalith Pellallawortha,
Buzzavean Chyponds Boswase,
Ventongimps Roskestal Raftra,
Hendra Grancan Treen Bostraze.

Treganebris Embla Bridgia,
Menadarva Trevencage,
Tregaminion Fouge Trevidgia,
Gwarnick Trewy Reskajeage.

Luggans Vellanvoane Treglisson,
Gear Noongumpus Helan gove,
Carnequidden Brea Bojoucan,
Drym Chykembra Dowran Trove.

Menagwithers Castlegotha,
Carnongrease Trevespanvean,
Prazeanbeeble Maen Trebarva,
Bone Trengwainton Lethargwean.

Stablehobba Balaswhidden,
Tringey Trannack Try Trenear,
Fraddam Crowlas Gwallan Crankan,
Drift Bojedna Cayle Trebear.

Haltergantic Carnaliezy,
Gumford Brunion Nancekeage,
Reen Trevesken Mevagizzy,
Killow Carbus Carn Tretheage.

THE next specimen is quoted from DR. BANNISTER'S *Glossary of Cornish Names*, wherein he says: "But what can be more melodious than the following string of names just put into a sort of song, or nonsense verse, though every name is significant, by old Mr. Le Grice, copied as here given, except the punctuation, from a very old manuscript:

"KARNEQUIDEN, Polpenhenna;
Wheallandruckia, Barlewenna;
Tregavarah, Treen, Chikembra;
Tolpednpenwith, Pendrea, Hendra;
Karnkie, Nudjack, Garledinnia;
Menedarva, Vellanhoggan;
Merther Uny, Tregaminion;
Amalveor, Polgoon, Bosahan;

Tregonebris, Begiltuban;
Hallywidden, Walcrouswoola;
Trelawarren, Parkanskeba;
Clies, Tregerthen, Ambejuah;
Praesanbygle, Vellanvoane;
Ponsanooth, Bostraze, Tretane;
Amalveor, Drulas, Treneere;
Skilewadden, Bougeheere;
Pednavounder, Gwills, Carnjue;
Trereef, Pednpons, Goongumpus, Treu;
Pednaventon, Trewjevean;
Chun, Carngwavas, Uskajean;
Embla, Chipons, Gwalancrane;
Ponsandain, Trengwainton Carne;
Drimbejowa, Crousanvra;
Killeankar, Boen, Trembah."

The Half-peeled Turnip.

E. A. DREWE (Major), Exeter. This and the following piece are from two volumes of *Poems by Gentlemen of Devonshire and Cornwall*, published at Exeter in 1792. This "pastoral ballad" is written in ridicule of Shenstone.

THE rain it is coming down fast,
　　The frogs they are hopping around;
　　The season of drought it is past,
The earth-worms crawl out of the ground.

The ants, that so crept up the trees,
    Are all now retired to their nest;
Snug in hive stay the flower-loving bees,
    'Tis holiday all, and 'tis rest :

The rook no more caws in the grove,
    Nor the wood-dove she maketh her moan;
All dull is the season of love,
    And Corydon's pleasure is flown :
For Phillis had promised to meet
    All down in the dew-sprinkled vale;
But he saw not the prints of her feet,
    He saw not the marks of her pail :

The rain had kept Phillis at home,
    To catch a sad cold was her fear;
Her mother forbade her to roam,
    So she sat by the fire in her chair.
Sad Corydon put on his hat,
    And hied him away to her house;
At the door he espied the loved cat—
    The cat had been seeking a mouse.

"Pretty pussy," says he, "are you wet?
    Alas! let me open the door;
Were I, like fond pussy, a pet,
    My breast would feel sorry no more!"

The cat he did cock up his tail,
    He purred, and he rubbed on his leg :
"Dear pussy! ah, could I prevail,
    One favour of thee would I beg.

"Go purr, and go rub on my love,
    By mewing express what I feel ;
Oh, try that hard bosom to move !
    I'll give thee a supper of eel."
As Phillis now sat by the fire,
    She heard the fond shepherd complain,
And kindly said, "Swain, I desire
    That you will come out of the rain."

He caught up the cat in his arms,
    Her summons so proud to obey ;
For Phillis, dear Phillis, had charms,
    And so all the shepherds would say.
"Dear Phillis," says he, "how d'ye do?"
    As soon as she heard the swain speak,
"Kind shepherd," says she, "how are you?"
    And the blushes they covered her cheek.

"Ah! why would you stay at the door?
    Ah! why in the rain would you wait?
See the poker, it lies on the floor ;
    Pray stir up the coals in the grate."

"Ah! why should I poke up the fire?
　Or why should I stir up the coal?
What is coal to my ardent desire?
　What is fire to the fire of my soul?

"So would flame yonder new-made hay-stack,
　If with candle the hay you should touch;
So the kidney be scorched, and turn black,
　Which the cook-maid has griddled too much;
So the cook-maid, if spit will not turn,
　Will roast on one side all her meat;
So, with frost aching, chilblains will burn,
　Which little girls have on their feet."

"Oh talk not of chilblains!" she cries,
　"But aid me, kind shepherd, I pray;
This turnip my patience defies;
　It will not be peeled to-day.
Ah, shepherd! if love sway thy breast,
　By this fond request I shall see;
Oh, give my tired fingers some rest!
　And peel the tough turnip for me."

He took out his knife in a trice—
　The knife that was crooked and keen;
He gave the turnip a slice—
　A slice such as never was seen:

The turnip was peeled well-nigh;
    The mother was feeding the hogs;
When, ah! she returned from the sty,
    The swain knew the sound of her clogs!

All hurried he ran out of door,
    And took not his hat in his hand;
The turnip rolled down on the floor,
    And Phillis was quite at a stand.
Home went Corydon, heartily soaked;
    Poor Phillis was lock'd up in spite;
So the fire it no longer was poked,
    Nor the turnip was peeled for the night!

To the Lark on Dartmoor.

— EMETT, Exeter, from the work last quoted.

SWEET soaring minstrel of the wild, I hear
    The pleasing music of thy tuneful throat,
As welcome o'er the desert to mine ear
    As to benighted hinds the matin note.
I thank thee, warbler, for thy cheering lay;
    But why in such a barren, lonely dell,
While other scenes their vernal sweets display,
    A winged recluse art thou content to dwell?
Oh, yet I trace the motives in thy song;
For freedom now the lofty burthen bears,

And now a tenderer strain is poured along,
And love is breathed with all its charming cares.
　　Thus, though e'en here sequestered, dost thou prove
Life's dearest blessings—Liberty and Love.

All for the Best.

Rev. John Swete, Oxton, Devon.

TWO friends by chance together met,
　　Who long had lived, and far asunder;
　　And while they took a morning's whet
They told such news as raised their wonder.
But now from politics and powers majestic
Their converse dropped, and turned on things domestic.

Says Hodge, "How fares it with you, friend?
　　I hope as how you're in a state of thriving."
"Why, since we parted I've had much to spend,
　　And that I got without much care by wiving."
"Ah! that looks well." "Nay, not so good:
　　The wife I wedded was a cursed scold."

"That truly might all other joys exclude."
　　"Not so; for she was worth her weight in gold."
"Well, there indeed you had your consolation;
For wealth will doubtless heal the worst vexation."
　　"Would that it had so happened; but, alas!
　　Fate otherwise decreed. It came to pass

That with her cash I bought a numerous flock.
  Then farmer turned : I ranged my fertile plains,
  And, buoyed with hope, I counted countless gains;
The murrain came, and perished all my stock."

"Good lack! Good lack! nay, that indeed's distressing."
  "Nay, not so bad; in every ill's a blessing.
You little think it, yet your wonder'll cease
When I inform you from the woolly fleece
  I even had a full redressing."

"Indeed! well, that was lucky! Fortune sure
Hath now been kind, and made your state secure."

"Ah, no! one night, one fatal night,
My sorrows reached their utmost height :
Ere from the market I could home return,
My goods, my houses, and my cattle burn."

"Alas! my friend, the Fates have spun thy threadful;
Sure, never yet was heard a case so dreadful."
" Why, so at first 'twould seem; but yet, believe me,
Kind fortune now did most of all relieve me;
What, can't you guess? Why, odd's my life!
With house and goods and cattle burnt—my wife!"

Marriage is Like a Devonshire Lane.

J. MARRIOTT, sometime vicar of Broadclyst.

N a Devonshire lane, as I trotted along
T' other day, much in want of a subject for song,
Thinks I to myself, I have hit on a strain;
Sure, marriage is much like a Devonshire lane.

In the first place, 'tis long, and when once you are in it,
It holds you so fast as a cage does a linnet;
For howe'er rough and dirty the road may be found,
Drive forward you must, there is no turning round!

But though 'tis so long, it is not very wide;
For two are the most that together can ride;
And e'en then 'tis a chance but they get in a pother,
And jostle and cross, and run foul of each other.

Oft Poverty greets them with mendicant looks,
And Care pushes by them, o'erladen with crooks;
And Strife's grazing wheels try between them to pass,
And Stubbornness blocks up the way on an ass.

Then the banks are so high, to the left hand and right,
That they shut up the beauties around them from sight!
And hence, you'll allow, 'tis an inference plain,
That marriage is just like a Devonshire lane.

But, thinks I too, these banks within which we are pent
With bud, blossom, and berry are richly besprent;
And the conjugal fence, which forbids us to roam,
Looks lovely when decked with the comforts of home.

In the rock's gloomy crevice the bright holly grows,
The ivy waves fresh o'er the withering rose;
And the evergreen love of a virtuous wife
Soothes the roughness of care, cheers the winter of life.

Then long be the journey, and narrow the way,
I'll rejoice that I've seldom a turnpike to pay;
And, whate'er others say, be the last to complain,
Though marriage is just like a Devonshire lane.

St. Aubyn Election Song.

This song, for a copy of which I am indebted to the Rev. C. M. Edward-Collins, of Trewardale, was evidently written in 1790, when Sir John St. Aubyn, grandfather of the present baronet, contested the county with Mr. F. Gregor, unsuccessfully. The St. Aubyn alluded to in the first stanza was the one of whom Walpole said that he knew the price of every man in the House of Commons except the little Cornish baronet. The tune is the old favourite "Vicar of Bray."

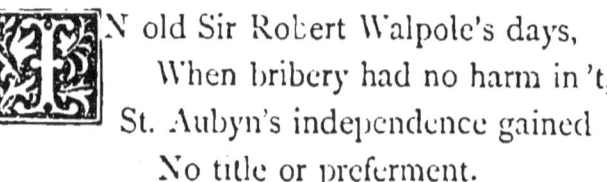
N old Sir Robert Walpole's days,
   When bribery had no harm in't,
St. Aubyn's independence gained
   No title or preferment.

He daily to Sir Robert said
  It was not his intention
His country or his rights to sell,
  And he despised a pension.

  And this is law he did maintain
    Unto his dying day, sir,
  His independence he would keep,
    Whatever Courtiers say, sir.

For Cornwall's trust his grandson asks,
  His pride! his wish! his glory!
And, this obtained, whatever tasks
  Ye set him, I'll assure ye,
If honour and integrity
  Give them a good foundation,
He'll do the best that do he may
  To serve ye and the nation.

  And this is law he did maintain
    Unto his dying day, sir,
  His independence he would keep,
    Whatever Courtiers say, sir.

Then let us one and all, my lads,
  Place in him our reliance;
His father's and his grandsire's work
  Calls loudly for affiance.

St. Aubyn's heir we'll then support—
It is our declaration—
Against the Lords, against the Court,
And every usurpation.

And this is law we will maintain
Unto our dying day, sir,
Sir John St. Aubyn we'll support,
Whatever Courtiers say, sir;
Our independence we'll support,
Whatever Courtiers say, sir.

Coplas de Jorge Manrique.

SIR JOHN BOWRING (1792-1872), born at Exeter, was a voluminous writer in various departments of literature, and the greatest linguist to whom the West of England has given birth. In addition to writing original poetry, he executed poetical translations from every European and all the principal Oriental languages. *Coplas de Jorge Manrique* is a translation from the Spanish, too long to quote in its entirety. The author died in 1479.

AWAKE, awake, my sleeping soul!
Rouse from thy dreams of hope and fear,
And think and see
How soon life's busy moments roll,
How soon the hour of death draws near,
How silently!

How swiftly hurrying joy glides by,
   And nought but sorrow's shade remains
      Of vanished bliss:
And sweeter is the memory
   Of other moments' griefs and pains,
      Than joys in this.

*   *   *   *

Our lives are rivers flowing on
   To that interminable sea,
      The mighty grave;
There go, as there have ever gone,
   All pomp and pride and royalty,
      Which nought can save.
There roll the mountain's rapid streams,
   There rolls the little gentle rill,
      There mingle all:
Lost in that ocean tide, which seems
   To swallow, though unsated still,
      The great, the small.

*   *   *   *

This world is but a narrow road
   That leads us to our home of rest,
      Far, far from woe:
So let us march to rest's abode,
   And choose our path, the straightest, best,
      While on we go.
Our birth begins our pilgrimage,
   And life is but our onward way;

Our journey's o'er
When we have reached the goal of age,—
We find the mansion of decay,
And tire no more.

And yet this idle world may be
A blessing and a glory, held
For what 'tis worth;
Since on the wings of piety
A well-trained soul may be impelled
To heaven from earth.
As God's high Son, inspired by love,
Descended from His mighty throne,
And dwelt with men,
And died, our souls may soar above,
And, welcomed by the Holy One,
Be blest again.

Oh, could we but adorn the face,
The corporal face, with skilful art
And beauty rare,
As we might clothe with glorious grace
And angel charms our brighter part,
And all that's fair!
Oh, what industrious, busy will,
What passion and what ardour we
Should bring to deck
The sensual captive with our skill,
While the bright soul of liberty
Might go to wreck!

And mark of what delusive worth
  The fleeting things for which we sigh,
    Satisfied never;
For in this vain, deceitful earth
  We lose them e'en before we die—
    Yes, lose for ever;
And time destroys them in its way—
  Vicissitude and accident,
    And busy change,
All bear the seeds of self-decay;
  And o'er the heights most eminent
    The tempests range.

Oh, tell me, tell me, beauty's cheek—
  Its mingling charms, its rosy hues,
    Its fragrant breath—
Where shall your vain enquiries seek
  When youth retires and age pursues,
    And levelling death?
The busy thoughts, the active will,
  The strength of youth—when youth is strong -
    When tottering age
Comes stumbling onward weak and chill,
  And fears, innumerable throng,
    Crowd on life's stage?

The azure Gothic blood, the line
  Of ancestry of long descent
    Of noble birth,

Through thousand paths its steps decline,
   And all that's proud and excellent
      Is swept to earth.
Some sink from native vileness; some
   From power that crushes them to dust
      In fortune's spite;
Some skilled in man erect their home
   In palaces of power and trust,
      And laugh at right.

But let them laugh; for trust and power,
   Of all deceitful shifting things,
      The most deceive;
They are the dewdrops of an hour
   Which fortune sweeps on restless wings,
      Pleased to bereave;
They are the dust which fortune throws
   From off her ever-whirling wheel
      While rolling on.
It sports with human weal and woe;
   It cannot rest; it ne'er stands still;
      It comes; 'tis gone.

   *   *   *   *   *

We read of mighty monarchs driven
   From highest pomp to low distress
      In ancient days;
Their sceptres and their glories riven,
   Their strength reduced to helplessness,
      And dimmed their praise.

Death treats all mortal things the same,
   And pope and prelate, king and count
      Alike he shocks;
He heeds no rank, respects no name,
   Calls or a shepherd on the mount,
      Or senseless flocks.

The Trojans are in darkness laid,
   And all they thought and all they did,
      Their losses—gains;
The Roman's history veiled in shade,
   That towered as towers a pyramid,
      But nought remains:
Why should we seek the vain display
   Of distant ages, treasured out
      In memory's hold,
When the events of yesterday
   Are vanished all—are all forgot—
      As deeds of old?

Where is King Juan—tell me, where?
   The Infantes, where, of Arragon,
      And all their deeds?
Where many a splendid cavalier,
   And many a nymph, and many a don,
      And stately steeds,
And jousts and tourneys; many a crest,
   And ornaments and arms of gold,
      And vizored brow?

They were a feverish dream at best,
  A wreath with flowerets manifold,
    All faded now.

Where are the proud and lofty dames,
  Their jewelled crowns, their gay attire,
    Their odours sweet?
Where are the love-enkindled flames,
  The bursts of passionate desire
    Laid at their feet?
Where are the songs, the troubadours,
  The music which delighted them?
    It speaks no more.
Where is the dance that shook the floors,
  And all the gay and laughing train,
    And all they wore?

  * * * *

The royal gifts profusely shed,
  The palaces so proudly built,
    With riches stored;
The roof with shining gold o'erspread,
  The services of silver gilt,
    The secret hoard,
The Arabian pards, the harness bright,
  The bending plumes, the crowded mews,
    The lacquey train,—
Where are they? where?—all lost in night,
  And scattered as the early dews
    Across the plain.

  * * * *

So many a lofty titled name,
   So many a marquis, duke, and count
      Of proud renown,
High lifted on the rolls of fame,
   Thou, Death, hast hurled from fortune's mount,
      And tumbled down!
Where hast thou hid them, Death? Those deeds
   Of peace serene, of sanguine war—
      All buried, lost:
Thy hand misguides, thy path misleads,
   Thy might destroys and scatters far
      Their pride and boast.

Their war battalions threatening round,
   Pennons and flags, and standards tall,
      Which thought ne'er told;
The watery moat, the guarded mound,
   Castle, portcullis, gate, and wall,
      And banner bold;
The sheltering trench, the deep-dug cave
   Made for retreat,—what serve they now,
      When death has sped
His mortal arrow from the grave,
   And tried his string and bent his bow
      For other dead?

Thou dost begin thy path with tears,
   And end that path with bitterness
      And labour vain:

Toil is the lot of middle years;
　The more of age, the more distress:
　　Most years, most pain;
Our joys just dawn when we decay:
　Gathered with sweat, and quickly gone,
　　And soon forgot.
Woes come on rapid wings, and stay,
　Tormenting still, and lingering on:
　　They vanish not.

Oh, World! thou practised in deceit,
　Were that vain life which thou dost give
　　But life indeed!
But, ah! it has no joy so great
　As when it bids us cease to live,
　　And says, "God speed."
For life is but a desert rude,
　Covered with darkness, filled with rocks,
　　And thorns, and woes,
Where 'tis in vain to look for good;
　For sorrow frowns and misery shocks,
　　And grief o'erflows.

To a Swallow.

NATHANIEL HOWARD, born at Plymouth, a schoolmaster at Tamerton Foliot. He was well versed in Persian, and translated much Persian poetry.

WITTERING tenant of the sky,
Whither, whither wilt thou fly?
Summer blithely frolics round;
Florid beauties grace the ground:
Rosy odours, youthful gales
Still breathe from bowers and verdurous vales.

Whither, fluttering, wilt thou fly,
Swiftest courser of the sky?
Still in brook or fountain spring
Dip thy never-weary wing;
Sweep along the level mead,
Where fragrant herds securely feed.

Happy vagrant, ever free,
All my fancies follow thee;
Mount with thee the blue serene,
Visit every foreign scene!
And, while seasons vary here,
With thee share summer all the year.

Whither, whither wilt thou fly,
Swiftest courser of the sky?

Stay, oh stay, till autumn's hand
Purple o'er my native land;
Mildness, health, and beauty, rove,
And fellow-warblers charm the grove.

Oh Keep thy Songs for Me!

FRANCIS HINGESTON (1796-1841), born at St. Ives. His poems, which are chiefly of an amatory character, were edited and published by his son, the Rev. F. C. Hingeston-Randolph, in 1857.

H keep thy songs for me, my love,
    Oh keep thy songs for me,
And I will keep my heart, my love,
    I'll keep my heart for thee!

If others bid thee smile, my love,
    If others bid thee smile,
Oh tell them thou art sad, my love,
    And I'll be sad the while!

If others come to woo, my love,
    If others come to woo,
Oh say that I'm thy slave, my love,
    And I will say so too!

Thy songs, thy smiles, thy sighs, my love,
    Oh keep them all for me;
My heart is all I have, my love,
    I'll keep it all for thee!

The Chant of the Brazen Head.

WINTHROP MACKWORTH PRAED (1801-1839), born in London, but bred in Devon, and of an old Cornish stock. He stands in the first rank of English writers of society verse, and mingled most happily humour, sarcasm, and pathos.

THINK, whatever mortals crave
  With impotent endeavour—
A wreath,—a rank,—a throne,—a grave—
  The world goes round for ever;
I think that life is not too long,
  And therefore I determine
That many people read a song
  Who will not read a sermon.

I think you've look'd through many hearts,
  And mused on many actions,
And studied man's component parts,
  And nature's compound fractions;
I think you've picked up truth by bits
  From foreigner and neighbour;
I think the world has lost its wits,
  And you have lost your labour.

I think the studies of the wise,
  The hero's noisy quarrel,
The majesty of woman's eyes,
  The poet's cherished laurel,

And all that makes us lean or fat,
    And all that charms or troubles,—
This bubble is more bright than that,
    But still they all are bubbles.

I think the thing you call Renown,
    The unsubstantial vapour,
For which the soldier burns a town,
    The sonnetteer a taper,
Is like the mist which, as he flies,
    The horseman leaves behind him;
He cannot mark its wreaths arise,
    Or if he does, they blind him.

I think one nod of mistress Chance
    Makes creditors of debtors,
And shifts the funeral for the dance,
    The sceptre for the fetters;
I think that Fortune's favour'd guest
    May live to gnaw the platters,
And he that wears the purple vest
    May wear the rags and tatters.

I think the Tories love to buy
    "Your Lordships" and "your Graces"
By loathing common honesty,
    And lauding common-places;

I think that some are very wise,
    And some are very funny,
And some grow rich by telling lies,
    And some by telling money.

I think the Whigs are wicked knaves,
    And very like the Tories,
Who doubt that Britain rules the waves,
    And ask the price of glories;
I think that many fret and fume
    At what their friends are planning,
And Mr. Hume hates Mr. Brougham
    As much as Mr. Canning.

I think that friars and their hoods,
    Their doctrines and their maggots,
Have lighted up too many feuds,
    And far too many faggots;
I think, while zealots fast and frown,
    And fight for two or seven,
That there are fifty roads to town,
    And rather more to Heaven.

I think that, thanks to Paget's lance,
    And thanks to Chester's learning,
The hearts that burned for fame in France,
    At home are safe from burning;

I think the Pope is on his back,
  And, though 'tis fun to shake him,
I think the Devil not so black
  As many people make him.

I think that Love is like a play,
  When tears and smiles are blended;
Or like a faithless April day,
  Whose shine with shower is ended;
Like Colnbrook pavement, rather rough;
  Like trade, exposed to losses;
And like a Highland plaid, all stuff,
  And very full of crosses.

I think the world, though dark it be,
  Has aye one rapturous pleasure,
Concealed in life's monotony,
  For those who seek the treasure;
One planet in a starless night,
  One blossom on a brier,
One friend not quite a hypocrite,
  One woman not a liar!

I think poor beggars court St. Giles,
  Rich beggars court St. Stephen;
And Death looks down with nods and smiles,
  And makes the odds all even;

I think some die upon the field,
   And some upon the billow,
And some are laid beneath a shield,
   And some beneath a willow.

I think that very few have sighed,
   When Fate at last has found them,
Though bitter foes were by their side,
   And barren moss around them;
I think that some have died of drought,
   And some have died of drinking;
I think—that nought is worth a thought,
   And I'm a fool for thinking!

A New Ballad

ABOUT ROBIN HOOD, BRIAREUS, AND THE GIANT GOG,

Showing who is a greater person than all three, and why.

W. M. PRAED. This is one of a series of election squibs, written in 1832, when Praed contested St. Ives with Mr. James Halse. This gentleman, who won the election, said that these squibs were "such trash that I am sure no gentleman will take the trouble to read them." After the election, Praed collected and published them, under the name of "Trash," dedicating the pamphlet, "without respect," to Halse. The "New Ballad" is one of the best. It is quoted as an illustration of Praed's facility in "squibbing," and of course without the slightest intention of expressing an opinion as to the merits of the matters in controversy. The allusion in the burden is to the fact that Halse charged Praed with being supported dictatorially by his land-tithe owning friends, Halse himself being taken to represent the tithe of fish yet levied in some parts of Cornwall. The "hands" in the second stanza are Halse's votes. "Trash" is now very scarce.

ROBIN HOOD was an archer good,
    No better was found in story;
    There never were days in the gay greenwood
        Like the days of Robin's glory.
Though swift on the wind were the wild deer's spring,
    Brave Robin's shaft outflew him;
Though high as the clouds were the falcon's wing,
    Brave Robin's bolt went through him.
A long, long bow did Robin bear;
    But when to St. Ives you go, sir,
They'll show you, I swear, a stout man there,
    Who shoots with a longer bow, sir.
        James Halse will be a fine M.P.,
            His zeal is vastly hot;
        "The tithe of corn is bad," quoth he,
        "And the tithe of fish is not."

Great Briareus had a hundred arms,
    As ancient poets tell us;
He shook high Heaven with fierce alarms,
    And made great Jupiter jealous.
He could pierce you at once with five score blades,
    If ever you prove refractory;
And practise at once some dozen of trades—
    A walking manufactory.

These limbs were long and huge and strong,
  But our hero might defy 'em;
For many more to him belong
  At a shilling or so per diem.
      James Halse will be a fine M.P.,
        His zeal is vastly hot;
      "The tithe of corn is bad," quoth he,
      "And the tithe of fish is not."

The giant Gog was a gluttonous dog,
  Enormous jaws he boasted;
He made but a mouthful of a hog,
  Whether 'twere raw or roasted:
For dinner he eat a fat ox up,
  And a tender calf for luncheon;
And he swilled at a sup in a silver cup,
  A hogshead or a puncheon.
But here in the West a man is found
  With an appetite far more funny;
When Wellesly sent five hundred pound,
  He swallowed all the money.
      James Halse will be a fine M.P.,
        His zeal is vastly hot;
      "The tithe of corn is bad," quoth he,
      "And the tithe of fish is not."

Alternatives.

JOHN KITTO, D.D. (1804-1854), born at Plymouth,
the "deaf author."

WERE all the beams that ever shone,
    From all the stars of day and night,
Collected in one single cone,
    Unutterably bright,
I'd give them for one glance of heaven
Which might but hint of sin forgiven.

Could all the voices and glad sounds
    Which have *not* fallen on my sense,
Be rendered up in one hour's bounds—
    A gift immense!—
I'd for one whisper to my heart
Give all the joy this might impart.

If the great deep now offered all
    The treasures in her bosom stored,
And at my feet I could now call
    That mighty hoard,
I'd spurn it utterly for some
Small treasure in the world to come.

If the sweet scents of every flower—
    Each one of which cheers more than wine—
One plant could from its petals pour,
    And that were mine,

I would give up that glorious prize
For one faint breath from Paradise.

Were all the pleasures I have known,
  "So few, so very far between,"
Into one great sensation thrown—
    Not then all mean—
I'd give it freely for one smile
From Him who died for me erewhile.

Memory.

J. F. Stevens. From *Fancy's Wreath*, published at Plymouth, 1821.

EM'RY! what is it? 'Mongst roses a briar—
  A pang amid pleasures—a sorrow in joy—
  A sigh while we're smiling—a check to desire—
A loss when we're gaining—a general alloy.

But if we reverse it? 'Mongst briars a rose—
  In pain 'tis a pleasure—a joy in distress—
A smile as we're sighing—a gain whilst we lose—
  It mars disappointment—makes sorrow grow less.

The Ride to Sea.

On the door of Haccombe Church, in Devon, are a couple of horse-shoes. The following ballad, written by a master of the Exeter Grammar School early in the present century, tells the traditional story concerning them.

THE feast was over in Haccombe Hall,
And the wassail cup had been served to all,
When the Earl of Totnes rose from his place,
And the chanters came in to say the grace.

But scarce was ended the holy rite,
When there stepped from the crowd a valiant knight;
His armour bright and his visage brown,
And his name Sir Arthur Champernowne.

"Good Earl of Totnes, I've brought with me
My fleetest courser of Barbary;
And whether good or ill betide,
A wager with thee I mean to ride."

"No Barbary courser do I own;
But I have," quoth the Earl, "a Devonshire roan;
And I'll ride for a wager, by land or sea,
The roan 'gainst the courser of Barbary."

"'Tis done!" said Sir Arthur, "already I've won;
And I'll stake my manor of Dartington

'Gainst Haccombe Hall and its rich domain."
So the Earl of Totnes the wager hath ta'en.

* * * * *

The land is for men of low degree;
But the Knight and the Earl they ride by sea.

"To horse! to horse!" resounds through the hall,
Each warrior steed is led from its stall;
And with gallant train over Milburn Down
Ride the bold Carew and the Champernowne.

And when they came to the Abbey of Tor,
The Abbot came forth from the western door,
And much he prayed them to stay and dine;
But the Earl took nought save a goblet of wine.

Sir Arthur he raised the bowl on high,
And prayed to the Giver of victory;
Then drank success to himself on the course,
And the sops of the wine he gave to his horse.

Away they rode from the Abbey of Tor
Till they reached the inlet's curving shore;
The Earl plunged first in the foaming wave,
And was followed straight by Sir Arthur the brave.

The wind blew hard and the waves beat high,
And the horses strove for the mastery;
Till Sir Arthur cried, "Help, thou bold Carew!
Help, if thou art a Christian true!

"Oh save for the sake of that lady of mine!
Good Earl of Totnes, the manor is thine;
The Barbary courser must yield to the roan,
And thou art the Lord of Dartington."

The Earl his steed began to restrain,
And he seized Sir Arthur's horse by the rein;
He cheered him with words, and gave him his hand,
And he brought Sir Arthur safe to land.

Then Sir Arthur, with sickness and grief oppressed,
Lay down in the Abbey chambers to rest;
But the Earl he rode from the Abbey of Tor
Straight forward to Haccombe Chapel door.

And there he fell on his knees and prayed,
And many an *Ave Mary* he said;
Bread and money he gave to the poor,
And he nailed the roan's shoes to the chapel door.

Gaveston on Dartmoor.

THE author of this striking ballad was born at Plymouth, a son of Mr. A. B. Johns, artist. He became a Unitarian minister, and died of cholera in the midst of his labours among the poor, during a cholera visitation in Liverpool. This poem, written while the author resided at Crediton, was published in the *New Monthly*, then under Campbell's editorship. Campbell was so struck with it that on the night of its reception he walked up and down his room, continually repeating fragments. It is founded on a tradition that during one of his banishments Gaveston was concealed on Dartmoor. Clazey Well Pool, near Sheepstor, is the tarn described.

T WAS a stern scene that lay beneath
    The cold grey light of autumn dawn;
Along the solitary heath
    Huge ghost-like mists were drawn.

Amid that waste of loneliness
    A small tarn, black as darkness, lay,
Silent and still: you there would bless
    The wild coot's dabbling play.

But not a sound rose there—no breeze
    Stirred the dull wave or dusky sedge;
Sharp is the eye the line that sees
    'Twixt moor and water's edge.

Yet on this spot of desertness
    A human shape was seen;
It seemed to wear a peasant's dress,
    But not with peasant's mien.

Now swift now slow the figure paced
    The margin of the moorland lake,
Yet ever turned it to the East,
    Where day began to wake.

"Where lags the witch? she willed me wait
    Beside this mere at daybreak hour,
When mingling in the distance sate
    The forms of cloud and tor.

"She comes not yet; 'tis a wild place—
    The turf is dank, the air is cold;
Sweeter, I ween, on kingly dais,
    To kiss the circling gold;

"Sweeter in courtly dance to tell
    Love tales in lovely ears;
Or hear, high placed in knightly selle,
    The crash of knightly spears.

"What would they say, who knew me then,
    Teacher of that gay school,
To see me guest of savage men
    Beside this Dartmoor pool?"

He sat him down upon a stone—
    A block of granite damp and grey—
Still to the East his eye was thrown,
    Now colouring with the day.

He saw the first chill dawn-light fade—
    The crimson flush to orange turn—
The orange take a deeper shade,
    As tints more golden burn.

He saw the clouds all seamed with light,
　　The hills all ridged with fire;
He saw the moor-fogs rifted bright,
　　As breaking to retire.

More near he saw the down-rush shake
　　Its silvery beard in morning's air;
And clear, though amber-tinged, the lake
　　Pictured its green reeds there.

He stooped him by the water's side,
　　And washed his feverish brow;
Then gazed as if with childish pride
　　Upon his face below.

But while he looks, behold him start,
　　His cheek is white as death!
He cannot tear his eyes apart
　　From what he sees beneath.

It is the Witch of Sheepstor's face
　　That grows from out his own!
The eyes meet his—he knows each trace—
　　And yet he sits alone.

Scarce could he raise his frighted eye
　　To glimpse the neighbouring ground,
When round the pool—white, dense, and high—
　　A wreath of fog was wound.

Next o'er the wave a shiver ran
    Without a breath of wind;
Then smooth it lay, though blank and wan,
    Within its fleecy blind.

And o'er its face a single reed,
    Without a hand to guide it, moved;
Who saw that slender rush, had need
    More nerve than lance e'er proved.

Letters were formed as on it passed,
    Which still the lake retained;
And when the scroll you traced at last,
    The reed fell dead, the lines remained.

On them the stranger's fixed eyes cling,
    To pierce their heart of mystery:
"*Fear not, thou favourite of a king,*
    That humbled head shall soon be high."

He scarce had read, a sudden breath
    Swept o'er the pool, and rased the lines;
The fog dispersed, and bright beneath
    The breezy water shakes and shines.

He looked around, but none was near—
    The sunbeams slept on moss and moor;
No living sound broke on his ear—
    All looked as lonely as before.

What had he given that hour to see
　The meanest herdsman of the hill!
For, bright as seemed the prophecy,
　A shadow dimmed his spirit still.

And well it might! the wanderer there
　Had stood too near an English throne—
Had breathed too long in princely air:
　He was the banished Gaveston.

Again he turned—again he flew
　To the boy bosom of his king—
Trod the proud halls his vain youth knew,
　Heard woman's voice and minstrel's string.

But double was the story told
　By the dark words of evil power,
And not Plantagenet could hold
　The Fates back in their own dark hour.

Beside the block his thoughts recall
　That scene of mountain sorcery—
Too late! for high on Warwick wall
　In one brief hour his head must be

Oh, how should evil deeds end well!
Or happy fates be told from hell!

The Voice of Nature.

SOPHIE DIXON (died 1855), born in Plymouth; from *Castalian Hours*.

HERE is a glory on the dark, rough hill
    When the low sun his setting radiance throws;
There is a beauty seems wide space to fill
When the fair moon in stainless lustre glows;
    There is a charm in summer's mossy rose,—
A music in the gale, and in the rill
    That through its reeds with bubbling whisper flows;
There is a grandeur when the clouds unfold,
    And the dread Tempest's voice bursts forth, until
Man can but listen; while its thunderings, rolled
    'Mid the torn skies, arouse the answering main.
Oh, earth, air, ocean! wherefore should we seek
    Language save yours?—the Eternal's glorious fane,
Where oracles of heaven round us speak.

To Evening.

HENRY INCLEDON JOHNS, born and died at Devonport.

LOVE thy twilight hour, sweet Eve!
    Thy shadowy forms, thy deepening hues,
A solemn tone to feeling give,
    And calmness o'er the soul diffuse.

Earth bids her fragrant incense rise,
 The stream with sweeter murmur flows,
And woodlands pour their melodies
 To bless that hour of soft repose!

When down the western sky afar
 Day's lingering beams but faintly glow,
I love to watch each trembling star
 Steal forth to gem Night's darkened brow.

And while I mark their silent course,
 And muse upon their destiny,
I think, among that shining host,
 My happier home one day may be!

Epigrams.

WILLIAM ROBERT HICKS (1808-1868), born at Bodmin, a humourist of the first order. "It will be long before one will arise fit to tread in his shoes. In wit he was inferior to Theodore Hook; in humour he could not compare with Sidney Smith; but in the union of both qualities and in geniality of disposition he was second to none. As a *raconteur* he was unrivalled."—J. C. YOUNG.

ON THE MARRIAGE OF JOB WALL AND MARY BEST.

JOB wanting a partner, thought he'd be blest
If of all womankind he selected the Best:
For, said he, of all evils that compass the globe,
A bad wife would most try the patience of Job.
The Best then he chose, and made bone of his bone,
Though 'twas clear to his friends she'd be Best left alone;
For though Best of her sex, she's the weakest of all,
If 'tis true that the weakest must go to the Wall.

ON THE MARRIAGE OF MR. LOT AND MISS SALTER.

BECAUSE on her way she chose to halt,
Lot's wife, in the Scriptures, was turned into salt;
But though on her course *she* ne'er did falter,
This young Lot's wife, strange to say, was *Salter*.

The Resurrection and the Life.

ELIAS TOZER (1825-1873), born at Ivybridge, journalist.

"Changes of glorious light from moving boughs, songs of birds, scents from gardens, woods, and fields—or rather, from the one great garden of the whole cultivated island in its yielding time— penetrate into the cathedral, subdue its earthy odour, and preach the Resurrection and the Life." Last words of the last number of the *Mystery of Edwin Drood*, by Charles Dickens.

ING, happy bird, your joyful lay,
From budding bough and shooting spray;
With music sweet lead in the May.

In grove and woodland, erst so bare,
No glad sounds charmed the wintry air—
The brooding earth seemed 'prest with care;

But now old Winter's reign is o'er,
Dear Spring appears with gen'rous store
Of joy and beauty at our door.

Out from the gloom of silent night
The Ruling Will evolves the light,
And turneth dark things into bright.

E'en from the grave Hope springs anew,
Sad hearts to gladden and renew,
And in our path loved flowers to strew.

O Earth! with changes ever rife,
Thou teachest, 'mid much pain and strife,
The Resurrection and the Life!

Cramp Song.

WILLIAM JEFFERY PROWSE (1836–1870), born at Torquay, was a facile writer of society verse. This "Tramp Song" was published after his death by his friend Tom Hood—now, alas! also departed—in his *Annual*.

THOUGH down in yonder valley
    The mist is like a sea,
Though the sun is scarcely risen,
    There is light enough for me.
  For, be it early morning,
  Or be it late at night,
    Cheerily ring my footsteps,
        Right! Left! Right!

I wander through the woodland
  That hangs about the hill,
Hark! the cock is tuning
  His morning clarion shrill;

And, suddenly awaking,
From his nest amid the spray
Hurriedly now the blackbird,
Whistling, greets the day.
  And be it early morning, etc.

I gaze upon the streamlet,
As on the bridge I lean;
I watch its hurried ripples,
I mark its golden-green.
Oh! the men of the West are stalwart,
And the Western lasses fair,
And merrily breathes around me
The bracing upland air.
  And be it early morning, etc.

What Constitutes a Mine?

CHARLES CHORLEY, journalist, died at Truro, where he had long resided. 1874. This "parody of a paraphrase" refers to the disputes and law suits as to the rateability of mines, which at one time used to recur at each county sessions, and in respect to which it was long held—though, as it has since appeared, in error—that mines were not rateable. It was at length decided that the surface works of mines were rateable; but mines of tin, lead, and copper are now rated under a recent act of Parliament.

HAT constitutes a mine?
Not agent's home, nor ornate counting-house,
 Where bold adventurers dine;
Not shops where carpenter his art may use,

And smith his brawny arm ;
Not stable, nor material-house, nor mill,
    Nor shed to shield from storm,
    Nor floors, nor powder-house, nor useful rill ;
No—ore, deep-treasured ore,
Of power the adventurous foreigner to lure
    O'er many a hill and moor,
Sustained by hope rich profits to ensure ;
    Ore—copper, tin, or lead,
With well-sunk shaft, and ladder, lift, and beam ;
    And above all, is need
Of engine moved by wonder-working steam.
    These constitute a mine ;
And parish officers in vain debate,
    And lawyers cute combine,
Aught among these by sessions' law to rate.
    Counselled by statesmen sage,
When England's maiden-queen, in prudence great,
    Made law for pauper age,
Mines she exempted from the parish rate.
    Such was her parish law,
And nought were fairer for Cornubia's weal.
    Shall farmers then o'erawe ?
Or lawyers threaten us that law's repeal ?
    Since mines so rarely pay
Those sweet rewards we labour to ensure,
    'Tis folly to give way,
And pay unmurmuring to the parish poor.

Resurgam.

GEORGE FREDERICK JACKSON (1836-1869), born at Plymouth. This piece, suggested by a tombstone which bore only the word "*Resurgam*" and the date 1600, is from a volume of his poems, published after his decease by his brother.

"I SHALL ARISE"—Two hundred years
    Upon the grey old churchyard stone
These words remain; no more is said;
    The grand old moral stands alone,
Untouched, while all the seasons roll
    Around it; March winds come and go,
The long-gone twilights fall and fade,
    Or autumn's sunsets burn and glow.

"I shall arise"—O wavering heart,
    From this take comfort and be strong!
"I shall arise"—nor always grope
    In darkness, mingling right with wrong;
From tears of pain, from shades of doubt,
    And wants within that blindly call,
"I shall arise"—in God's own light
    Behold the sum and truth of all.

What though I strove and could not reach
    The prize of love and truth I sought,
The grasp of longer life, the calm
    Of broader faith, of wider thought?

This is not all—not all? the germ
    Alone of what is yet to be :
Like children here we wade the shoals,
    And far out lies the vast of sea :

Like children yet we lisp in life,
    And till the perfect manhood, wait
At home our time, and only dream
    What lies beyond the outer gate :
God's full free universe of life—
    No shadowy paradise of bliss,
No realms of unsubstantial souls,
    But real,—life more true than this.

More true than this, nor all too changed
    And rose-ethereal; leaving scope
For simple blessings, tears of joy,
    God's gifts of Faithfulness and Hope :
Not set so far from touch of Love
    And Love's communion, pure and sweet,
But we may draw like Mary near,
    And fall and kiss the Saviour's feet.

O soul ! where'er your ward is kept,
    In some still region calmly blest,
By quiet watch-fires till dawn comes,
    And God's reveillè break your rest;

O soul! who left this record here,
  I read, and scarce can read for tears;
I bless you, reach and clasp your hand,
  For all these long two hundred years.

" I shall arise," O clarion call!
  Time rolling onward to the end
Brings the sure truth that cannot die,
  The life where Faith and Knowledge blend;
Each after each the cycles roll
  In silence, and around us here
The shadow of the great White Throne
  Falls broader, deeper, year by year.

Ode to the North-East Wind.

CHARLES KINGSLEY (1819-1875), Vicar of Eversley and Canon of Westminster. Permission to include in the *Garland* this fine ode, from *Andromeda and other Poems*, was given by the lamented Canon not long before death bereft us of one of the best and noblest worthies of Devon—faithful minister, true poet, ripe scholar, stout and honest-hearted gentleman—one in whom the spirit of England's bravest days lived again, and who embodied the old glories in pages that will never die. Messrs. Macmillan, to whom the copyright of the poem belongs, kindly joined their consent to that of the author.

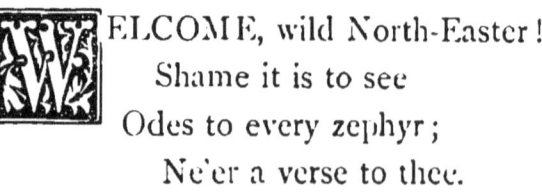ELCOME, wild North-Easter!
  Shame it is to see
Odes to every zephyr;
  Ne'er a verse to thee.

ODE TO THE NORTH-EAST WIND.

Welcome, black North-Easter!
   O'er the German foam,
O'er the Danish moorlands,
   From thy frozen home.
Tired we are of summer,
   Tired of gaudy glare,
Showers soft and steaming,
   Hot and breathless air.
Tired of listless dreaming
   Through the lazy day:
Jovial wind of winter,
   Turn us out to play.
Sweep the golden reed-beds,
   Crisp the lazy dyke;
Hunger into madness
   Every plunging pike.
Fill the lake with wild fowl;
   Fill the marsh with snipe;
While on dreary moorlands
   Lonely curlew pipe.
Through the black fir forest
   Thunder harsh and dry,
Shattering down the snow-flakes
   Off the curdled sky.
Hark! the brave North-Easter,
   Breast-high lies the scent,
On by holt and headland,
   Over heath and bent.

Chime, ye dappled darlings,
    Through the sleet and snow.
Who can override you?
    Let the horses go!
Chime, ye dappled darlings,
    Down the roaring blast;
You shall see a fox die
    Ere an hour be past.
Go and rest to-morrow,
    Hunting in your dreams,
While our skates are ringing
    O'er the frozen streams.
Let the luscious South wind
    Breathe in lovers' sighs,
While the lazy gallants
    Bask in ladies' eyes.
What does he but soften
    Heart alike and pen;
'Tis the hard grey weather
    Breeds hard English men.
What's the soft South-Wester?
    'Tis the ladies' breeze,
Bringing home their trueloves
    Out of all the seas:
But the black North-Easter,
    Through the snow-storm hurled,
Drives our English hearts of oak
    Seaward round the world.

Come as came our fathers,
Heralded by thee,
Conquering from the westward
Lords by land and sea.
Come, and strong within us
Stir the Viking's blood,
Bracing brain and sinew;
Blow, thou wind of God!

Trelawny; or, The Song of the Western Men.

R. S. HAWKER, vicar of Morwenstow, born at Plymouth. This is a song with a history. From the time when Bishop Trelawny was sent to the Tower by James II. with the other six Bishops, there had been current in Cornwall some fragments of an old ballad written on the occasion, which became very popular. One version of the burden ran—

"And shall they scorn Tre, Pol, and Pen?
And shall Trelawny die?
There's twenty thousand underground
Will know the reason why."

In 1825 Mr. Hawker wrote the song which follows, founded upon these fragments, and sent it to a Plymouth newspaper. When it was published, it at once attracted attention. Mr. Davies Gilbert thought it was the original old ballad, and had a number of copies privately printed and circulated. Scott, Macaulay, and later, Dickens, held the same view, and it was not until Mr. Hawker came forward and proved his authorship that its real origin was known. It is one of the most spirited compositions in the language. Mr. Hawker has published several volumes of poetry, chiefly dealing with Western subjects.

 GOOD sword and a trusty hand,
　　A merry heart and true!
King James's men shall understand
　　What Cornish lads can do.

And have they fixed the where and when?
　　And shall Trelawny die?
Here's twenty thousand Cornishmen
　　Will know the reason why.

Out spake their captain, brave and bold,
　　A merry wight was he—
"If London's tower were Michael's hold,
　　We'll set Trelawny free!

"We'll cross the Tamar, land to land,
　　The Severn is no stay,
With 'one and all,' and hand in hand,
　　And who shall bid us nay?

"And when we come to London wall,
　　A pleasant sight to view,
'Come forth, come forth, ye cowards all,
　　Here's men as good as you.'"

Trelawny lies in keep and hold,
　　Trelawny he may die,
But here's twenty thousand Cornish bold
　　Will know the reason why.

A Wish.

SIBELLA ELIZABETH HATFIELD, born at Falmouth.

LET not my life be like the stagnant lake,
    For ever sleeping in the sunny beam;
    I ask it not—no! rather let it make
A course like that of some fair mountain stream,
    Now rushing on its way with many a beam
Of sunny hope, now gliding through the mead
    Of verdant joy, and now (if Heaven deem
More useful) through the dark and lowly shade;
Though it be lost to sight, it still may verdure aid.

The Lady of Place.

HENRY SEWELL STOKES, Clerk of the Peace for the County of Cornwall, author of the *Vale of Lanherne* and numerous other poetical works. The Lady of Place was the wife of Thomas Treffry, and the incident occurred in 1457.

FIVE hundred years and more ago,
    Third Edward ruled us then,
  From Fowey near fifty ships set sail,
    With nigh eight hundred men:
No other port on England's coast
    An equal force could bring;
For Calais, when they weighed, they formed
    The vanguard of the King.

And when of Henries reigned the sixth
  The ships of Fowey went forth
To every sea and every shore,
  East, West, and South, and North,
And the bay was like a forest—
  For tall and stately masts
And flags of many countries
  Came with the veering blasts.

The Fowey men grew so haughty,
  They would no bonnet veil;
But the folk of Rye and Winchelsea
  Would make them dip the sail.
And on a day, to settle it,
  They fought both man and boy;
And from that time those Cornish lads
  Were called Gallants of Fowey.

Still they fell to merchandize,
  And prouder still they grew:
Their cruisers harassed all the coast
  From Cherbourg to Bordeaux.
But one dark night, when scattered far
  Their ships on ocean wide,
A sound as from a cloud of sails
  Came with the flowing tide.

The Lady of Treffry remained
  In her large mansion lone;

Her husband to the distant chase
    With horse and hound had gone.
The watch-dogs barked; then shouts, then shrieks
    Rose from the sleeping town:
The vengeful French, like unloosed fiends,
    Went ranging up and down.

Here torches flashed, there sledges crashed,
    Such was their devilish game;
And soon from many a house-top
    Burst out the crimson flame.
As in broad day men saw the bay,
    The ships, the stores, the towers;
And blinding clouds of smoke came down,
    And red flames fell in showers.

But she was there, that Lady,
    To play no woman's part;
Though the great sufferings of her town
    Had pierced her gentle heart:
And Fowey men, like a wall of steel,
    Though few, about her stood;
While some, to cut the ships adrift,
    Crept out upon the flood.

And on the wharves and in the streets
    Was heard the awful clang
Of swords and weapons strange; with fists
    Some on the Frenchmen sprang;

Some met them with a Cornish grip
  They never more forgot;
And many found the Cornish hug
  Much rougher than they thought.

But other were the scenes and sounds
  Of that unhappy night,
When, like a flock of bleating lambs,
  By the burning roof-trees' light,
Mothers their wailing children led
  Through wood and sheltered lane,
And by the winding moorland paths,
  Which to this day remain.

Still calm looked forth the Lady
  From her embattled wall;
Her presence was a power; her voice
  Thrilled like a trumpet's call.
Meanwhile the bells kept tolling,
  To rouse the country round;
And spires and turrets far away
  Sent on the warning sound.

And long before the daylight
  Fires lit the lofty peaks;
And men were moving in the vales,
  And stirring in the creeks.
Small need, so brave that Lady proved
  The Fowey gallants so true,

That at cock-crow, like baffled wolves,
    The Frenchmen all withdrew.

Whether a panic seized them
    I will not pause to learn;
They had done enough of mischief,
    And might perhaps return.
But when they went to find their ships
    The Fowey folk laughed outright;
For some were scuttled, some aground,
    Some drifting out of sight.

Next morning with his posse
    The Sheriff came at dawn;
The flames still roared, the French on board
    The ships they saved had gone:
Three cheers, then, for the Fowey gallants!
    For the Lady three times three!
And if the French should come again,
    May our wives as fearless be!

Changed is the world, much changed since then,
    Yet will they come once more?
Who knows, or cares, or fears? Who doubts
    We'll serve them as before?
Grace Darling died but yesterday,
    And others of her race
May yet be found to emulate
    That Lady brave of Place.

Tintagel.

NICHOLAS MICHELL, born at Truro. Mr. Michell is the most prolific of modern Western poets, and his writings, which include several poems of considerable length, have passed through numerous editions. "Ruins of Many Lands" is one of the best known of his larger works, and "Tintagel" is a good example of his shorter pieces. It is also one of his latest.

ATURE to famed Tintagel yields a glory
   In cliffs stupendous, breasting ocean's roar;
Cliffs, strong-armed giants ages have made hoary,
   Guarding wild Cornwall's shore.

History and legend make the spot around us
   Immortal, though dumb Solitude sits queen :
A chain of interest and deep awe hath bound us,
   Enchantment fills the scene.

Here, while we listen to the billows' thunder,
   Waves tossing, rolling, in their mad unrest,
Spray, like broad sheets of snow, a whitening wonder,
   Flung up from ocean's breast :

Fancy will see King Arthur's ghost, lone standing,
   Misty, gigantic, on yon beetling rock,
All cased in steel, as if some host commanding,
   Waiting the battle's shock.

TINTAGEL.

We see him now, his skeleton arms extending
    To where his castle stood, high-walled and strong,
Back over days of splendour, memory sending—
    Days of pomp, feast, and song.

He hears, upon the landward breezes swelling,
    The shouts of heroes, woman's laughter sweet—
All of his once-loved Cornish kingdom telling;
    His knights he seems to greet.

Poor ghost! he vanishes mid foam of ocean,
    His glittering mail, sword, spear, have passed away:
The tufted sea-pink, with a tremulous motion,
    Waves on his castle gray.

Bald stones his once grand fortress—let us listen!
    For battle-shouts and songs of ladies fair,
We hear the cormorant's cry where wet rocks glisten,
    And sea-weeds trail their hair.

In tiltyard and grassed keep the rabbit burrows,
    And, mid the wild-flowers, hums the reckless drone:
Below, the waves, in chasms and long furrows,
    Wear rocks, and dash and moan.

Grim Ruin folds her mantle, pensive sitting
    By crumbled walls; she cries, "The scene is mine!"
There Desolation's shade is nightly flitting,
    Shrieking, as moonbeams shine.

Yes, as the wan, pure light around is falling,
   Silvering the crags and ocean's tossing spray,
A voice from out the mouldered stones seems calling,
   "Thus pomp, power, melt away!"

Yet down the ages, O ye Rocks and Ocean!
   When cold this heart, and dim this raptured eye,
Pilgrims will seek yon shore in warm devotion,
   Pondering on years gone by.

When not a stone of Arthur's pile is frowning
   Above the waste of thundering waves below,
Song with its magic will these cliffs be crowning,
   Brightening the long ago :

'Gainst desolate rocks the billows will be dashing,
   But fancy shall place forms on crag and hill ;
And warm Romance, her bright eyes backward flashing,
   Halo Tintagel still.

River of Dart.

MORTIMER COLLINS, born at Plymouth. Mr. Collins is among the best-known writers of the day. He has published several volumes of charming poetry, and a number of novels. The poem quoted is founded on the current couplet with which it opens, and which embodies the popular belief that each year some one must be drowned in the stream addressed.

"RIVER of Dart! O river of Dart!
　　Every year thou claimest a heart."
　　　　Beautiful river, through fringe of fern
　　Gliding swift to the southern sea,
　　Such is the fame thy wild waves earn,
　　Such is the dirge men sing by thee:
For the cry of Dart is the voice of doom,
When the floods are out in the moorland gloom.

River of Dart! beside thy stream
In the sweet Devon summer I linger and dream;
　　For thy mystic pools are dark and deep,
　　　　And thy flying waters strangely clear,
　　And the crags are wild by the Lover's Leap,
　　　　And thy song of sorrow I will not hear,
While the fierce moor-falcon floats aloft,
And I gaze on eyes that are loving and soft.

River of Dart! the praise be thine
For the loving eyes that are meeting mine!
　　Where thy swift trout leap, and thy swallows dip,
　　　　'Neath a gray tor's shadow 'twas mine to know
　　The pure first touch of a virgin lip,
　　　　And the virgin pant of a breast of snow.
River of Dart! O river of Dart!
By thy waters wild I have found a heart.

Where hast thou been, my beautiful Spring?

EDWARD CAPERN, of Bideford, the Devonshire postman-poet. From the first volume of his poems, published while yet he was a rural postman.

HERE hast thou been, my beautiful Spring?
To the sultry south, on the swallow's wing;
Kissing the little kidnapped slave,
Ere borne away on the deep blue wave;
Brushing the tear from the mother's cheek,
As she wept for her child at Mozambique?
Else whence comest thou with this potent charm,
   Chaining the winds to the frozen zone,
Making the breast of Nature warm,
   And stilling old Winter's undertone?

Where hast thou been, my beautiful Spring?
Away with the honey-bee wandering,
Sipping the nectar of famed Cashmere,
Sporting amid the Turk's parterre,
Quaffing warm Araby's balmy breeze,
And spicy scents of the Ceylonese?
Else whence comest thou with thy odorous breath,
   Chafing the cheek to a rosy bloom,
And scattering the poisonous air of death
   By flinging abroad a rich perfume?

WHERE HAST THOU BEEN?

Where hast thou been, my beautiful Spring?
Up 'mid heaven's music revelling?
For the tones of that song from the greenwood bush,
The lark in the sky, and the mountain-thrush,
Speak as if it were given to thee
To list to seraphic minstrelsy.
Ay, there thou hast been. Not sunny France,
   Or old Italia's land of song,
Can furnish such notes for the poet's dance
   As the melody poured from thy musical tongue.

Where hast thou been, my beautiful Spring?
Plucking rich plumes from the paroquet's wing,
Robbing the clouds of their rainbow crest,
Bathing thyself in the glorious West,
Robing thy form in the peacock's hues,
And gathering pearls from the orient dews?
Else whence comest thou, with this proud array
   Of beauties to sprinkle the russet wood,
The Lent-lilies bending as if to pray,
   And hyacinths fringing the marge of the flood?

And tell me whence cometh, my beautiful Spring,
Each star of the earth, each odorous thing,
These white ruffled daisies with golden-dipped eyes,
These buttercups gleaming like summer-lit skies,
These violets adorned with rich purple and blue,
These primroses fragrant and innocent too,

And lastly, the sweetest and richest, I ween,
    Of all thy fair daughters, my beautiful Spring,
The buddings that stud all thy pathways with green;
    Say, where were they gathered to shake from thy wing?

Girt Ofvenders an' Zmal.

HENRY BAIRD, journalist. Mr. Baird has written much in the Devonshire dialect, under the *nom de plume* of "Nathan Hogg."

MULLER ha voun a mowze in ez hutch,
    An' zed, "Vur this yu bee bown ta dye;"
Bit tha pore litt'l crayt'r playdid hard,
    An' wanted ta naw tha rayz'n wye.

"Tha rayz'n wye?" tha muller ha zed,
    "Way that's a purty thing, ta be zshore;
Now wadd'n thee voun in thic thare hutch,
    A aytin tha mayl that's grownd vur tha pore?"

Then ha cort'n hole ba tha end a tha tayl,
    An' ez pore litt'l haid gin tha hutch ha hat,
Arter wich tha cruel twoad ha drade
    Ez pore litt'l carkiss owt ta tha cat.

Now a muller ha stayl'th, an' cal'th et "tole,"
    An' a mowthvul ur tu a mowze'll scral;
Wat a honjist vate thare ez, I zess,
    Vur ofvenders girt an' ofvenders zmal.

Grammer's Cat and Ours.

JOHN TABOIS TREGELLAS (1792-1865), born at St. Agnes. The greatest master of the niceties of the Cornish dialect, in which he wrote largely, both in prose and verse. The piece quoted from is included in a volume of miscellanies published by Mr. Netherton, Truro, and happily indicates the marked difference between the modern dialect of Cornwall and that of Devon, illustrated in "Girt Ofvenders an' Zmal." The hero of "Grammer's Cat" is a miner named Jim Chegwidden.

TO wash his hands and save the floshing,
Outside the door Jim did his washing,
But soon returned in haste and fright—
"Mother, aw come! and see the sight;
Up on our house theere's such a row,
Millions of cats es up theere now!"
Jim's mother stared, and well she might;
She knew that Jim had not said right.
"Millions of cats," you said; "now worn't it so?"
"Why iss," said Jim, "and I beleeve ut too;
Not millions p'rhaps, but thousands must be theere,
And fiercer cats than they you'll never hear;
They're spitting, yowling, and the fur is flying,
Some of em's dead, I s'pose, and some es dying;
Such desmal grooans I'm sure you never heerd,
Aw, mother! ef you ded, you'd be affeered."
"Not I," said Jinny; "no, not I, indeed;
A hunderd cats out theere, thee'st never seed."

Said Jim, " I doan't knaw zackly to a cat,
They must be laarge wauns then to do like that ;
They maake such desmal noises when they're fighting,
Such scrowling, and such tearing, and such biting."
" Count ev'ry cat," says Jinny, " 'round and 'round ;
Iss, rams and yaws, theer caan't be twenty found."
" We'll caall 'em twenty, mother, ef 'twill do ;
Shut all the cats, say I ; let's have my stew."
" No, Jimmy, no !—no stew to-night,
'Tell all the cats es counted right."

" Heere goes," said Jim ; " lev Grammer's cat go fust
(Of all the thievish cats, he es the wust).
You knaw Mal Digry's cat, he's nither black nor blue,
But howsomever, he's a cat, and that maakes two ;
Theere's that theere short-tailed cat, and she's a he,
Short tail or long now, mother, that maakes three ;
Theere's that theere grayish cat what stawl the flour,
Hee's theere, I s'pose, and that, you knaw, maakes fower ;
Trevenen's black es theere, ef he's alive,
Now, mother, doan't 'ee see, why that maakes five ;
That no-tailed cat, that waance was uncle Dick's,
He's surely theere to-night, and that maakes six ;
That tabby cat you gove to Georgey Bevan,
I knaw *hes* yowl—he's theere, and that maakes seven ;
That sickly cat we had, cud ait no mait,
She's up theere too to-night, and she maakes 'ight ;
That genteel cat, you knaw, weth fur so fine,
She's surely theere, I s'pose, and that maakes nine ;

Tom Avery's cat es theere, they caall un Ben,
A reg'lar fighter he, and he maakes ten;
The ould maid's cat, Miss Jinkin broft from Devon,
I s'pose she's theere, and that, you knaw, maakes 'leven;
Theere's Grace Penrose's cat, got chets, 'tes awnly two,
And they're too young to fight as yet; so they waan't do.
Iss, 'leven's all that I can mind,
Nor more than 'leven you waan't find;
So lev me have my supper, mother,
And let the cats ait one another."
  "No, Jimmy, no!
  It shaan't be so;
No supper shu'st thou have this night
Until the cats thee 'st counted right;
Go taake the lantern from the shelf,
And go and count the cats thyself."
 See hungry Jimmy with his light,
Turned out to count the cats aright;
And he who had Hugh Tonkin blamed
Did soon return, and, much ashamed,
Confessed the number was but two,
And both were cats that well he knew.
  Jim scratched his head,
  And then he said—
"Theere's Grammer's Cat and Ours out theere,
And they two cats made all that rout theere;
But ef two cats made such a row,
'Tes like a thousand, any how."

Impromptu Bruneliana.

On the day of the opening of the Royal Albert Bridge by the late Prince Consort, May 27th, 1859. R. R. B., Director of the Cornwall Railway.

T East and West of Britain's favoured isle
Two rivers flow, far deeper than the Nile;
At each a work of transcendental skill
All eyes attract, all minds with wonder fill.
The *Bridge* reared here, the *Tunnel* there, display
The under transit and the over way;
Each stands unrivalled in the science race,
That sapping chaos! *this* enchaining space!
So long as commerce shall her marts maintain,
And ocean towers denote Britannia's reign,
Shall *Thames* and *Tamar* the great genius own
Of Brunel Father and of Brunel Son.

St. Peter's Day at Polperro.

Anne Gibbons, *née* Trelawny, born at Penquite, wife of the Rev. G. B. Gibbons. Old St. Peter's Day is retained at Polperro, and its eve celebrated by the lighting of a huge bonfire, originally intended, according to Mr. Couch (*History of Polperro*), to celebrate the great solstitial feast.

THE ancient Druid worship lingers here!
The Bardic faith of Mona's haunted steep,
The torch-blaze glows, the kindling pile they
While pale Astarte lights the mysteries drear. [heap,

The shout is heard, the victim's frantic cry,
And curling smoke-wreaths shroud the smothering blaze.
Ah! mirthful now and harmless revelry!
Linked with the purer faith of Saxon days,
When Christian teachers sought the Cornish shore,
And wisely it may be with custom bore;
Nor banished, all too stern, the reverend rites
Once paid in error: now the feast invites
Of him who toiled on Galilee's dark lake,
And bowed to lowly death for Jesus' precious sake.

Helston Furry Day Song.

HELSTON has been noted for centuries for a singular festival, held on the 8th of May, the origin of which is disputed and doubtful. Early on the morning of that day the young folk go into the country to bring in the May—*i.e.* flowers and greenery. Later in the forenoon parties assemble and dance through the streets to a quaint traditional tune, following a traditional route, which takes them through houses and gardens. The dance is continued round the town until the dancers return to the starting-point— the "Angel Hotel"—where they dance upstairs into the ball-room, and there finish the measure. Sometimes there are several dancing parties. The leading families of the locality take part in the celebration; and in the evening there is a ball. The following is the song which is sung (not to the dance tune) by the May-seekers. Some parts are not easy of explanation; but the reference to the Spaniards clearly dates back to Elizabethan days. "Hale and tow" is a very ancient traditional burden.

ROBIN HOOD and Little John
   They both are gone to the fair, O !
And we will go to the merry greenwood
   To see what they do there, O ;
   And for to chase, O—
   To chase the buck and doe,
      With hale an tow, rum below ;
      For we were up as soon as day, O,
      And for to fetch the summer home,
      The summer and the may, O ;
      For summer is a come, O,
      And winter is a gone, O.

Where are those Spaniards
   That make so great a boast, O ?
They shall eat the grey goose feather,
   And we will eat the roast, O,
      In every land, O,
      The land where'er we go.

As for St. George, O,
   Saint George he was a knight, O ;
Of all the knights in Christendom,
   Saint Georgy is the right, O,
      In every land, O,
      The land where'er we go.

God bless Aunt Mary Moses,
   With all his power and might, O ;

And send us peace in merry England
Both day and night, O!
And send us peace in merry England
Both now and evermore, O!

The Padstow Hobby-horse Songs.

THE May-day celebration locally known as the Padstow Hobby-horse is clearly a relic of the ancient Guise or Morice Dancers; and the songs which are associated with it bear traces of great antiquity. One cannot fail to be struck with the almost entire identity of the second line of each stanza in the first "Summer is a come in (or comen) to-day," with the opening of that most ancient of English songs, "Summer is a comen in." The hobby-horse is a grotesque figure of a man dressed up in a mask and cocked-hat, and bestriding a stick with a rudely-carved horse's head, his legs being hidden by a kind of tarpaulin drapery, so as to carry out the hobby-horse idea as much as possible. The hobby-horse celebration begins on May-day eve, the youngsters of the town having been engaged as much as a week previously in digging the "May-pit" for the reception of the May-pole, which is decked and erected on May-day eve. The chief members of the hobby-horse party then pawn the horse. This ceremony is performed by taking supper at a chosen public-house, the cost of the meal having to be defrayed out of the succeeding day's receipts. After supper, and commencing about midnight, the party stroll through the town singing the first song, being especially heedful to render honour to their patrons by inserting their names in the blanks. About ten the next morning the hobby-horse makes his appearance, and is taken round the town to the discordant music, if music it may be called, of a heterogeneous collection of whistles, concertinas, drums, triangles, and tambourines, occasionally strengthened by engaging the services of an organ-grinder. At intervals a grotesque dance is gone through, and the second song is sung. Well-to-do people not many years ago took part in the festivity; but it is now rapidly falling into decay. After the horse is taken out of pawn, by paying for the supper, the money collected in the town and neighbourhood is shared.

A popular theory of the origin of the hobby-horse is that some centuries ago the French attempted a landing at Padstow, and that the inhabitants, not being strong enough to resist, got rid of them by a ruse, dressing all the women in red cloaks, and marching them, headed by Aunt Ursula Bird—celebrated as "Un (Cornish for aunt) Ursula Bird" in song number two—down to Park Cove, preceded by the hobby-horse, where they so frightened the French, who took them for soldiers led on by the devil, that they ran away. The red cloak story is told, however, of almost every place on the coast, and there is no special reason for fixing its actual locality at Padstow; whilst the hobby-horse is clearly of another origin. Still, the song may preserve the memory of some attack upon the town, though it and the hobby-horse festivity appear now to be hopelessly mixed. I am indebted for the copy of these interesting songs to Mr. M. Trebilcock.

NUMBER ONE.

UNITE! all unite! It's now all unite,
    For summer is a come in to-day;
    And whither we are going it's all now unite
In the merry morning of May.

With the merry singing and the joyful spring—
    For summer is a come in to-day—
How happy are those little birds that merrily doth sing
    In the merry morning of May!
        Chorus—Unite! all unite! &c.

Young men and maidens, I warn you every one—
 For summer is a come in to-day—
To go unto the green woods, and bring the may home
 In the merry morning of May.

Rise up, Mr. ——, with your sword by your side,
 For summer is a come in to-day;
Your steed is in the stable, and waiting for to ride
 In the merry morning of May.

Rise up, Mrs. ——, all in your gown of silk,
 For summer is a come in to-day—
And all your bodice under as white as any milk,
 In the merry morning of May.

Rise up, Mr. ——, and gold be your ring,
 For summer is a come in to-day;
And send to us a cup of ale, and better we shall sing
 In the merry morning of May.

Rise up, Mrs. ——, all in your gown of green,
 For summer is a come in to-day;
You are so fair a lady as waits upon the queen,
 In the merry morning of May.

Rise up, Mr. ——, and his bride by his side,
 For summer is a come in to-day;
For blithe is your bride that lays down by your side
 In the merry morning of May.

Rise up, Mr. ——. I know you well-a-fine,
    For summer is a come in to-day;
You have a shilling in your purse, but I wish it was in mine,
    In the merry morning of May.

Rise up, Miss ——, all out of your bed,
    For summer is a come in to-day;
Your chamber shall be strewed with the white rose and the red,
    In the merry morning of May.

Rise up, Miss ——, and strew all your flowers,
    For summer is a come in to-day;
It is but a while ago since we have strewed ours,
    In the merry morning of May.

Rise up, Miss ——, and reach to me your hand,
    For summer is a come in to-day;
You are so fair a damsel as any in the land,
    In the merry morning of May.

Rise up, Master ——, and reach me your hand—
    For summer is a come in to-day—
And you shall have a lively lass, and a thousand pounds in hand,
    In the merry morning of May.

Where are the maidens that here now should sing?—
 For summer is a come in to-day—
Oh, they are in the meadows the flowers gathering
 In the merry morning of May.

The young maids of Padstow, they might if they would—
 For summer is a come in to-day—
They might have made a garland, and decked it all in gold,
 In the merry morning of May.

Where are the young men that here now should dance?—
 For summer is a come in to-day—
Oh, some they are in England, and some they are in France,
 In the merry morning of May.

The young men of Padstow, they might if they would—
 For summer is a come in to-day—
They might have built a ship, and gilt her all in gold,
 In the merry morning of May.

Now fare ye well; we bid you all good cheer,
 For summer is a come in to-day;
We'll call once more unto your house before another year,
 In the merry morning of May.

[This last verse is sung as a conclusion to either a part or whole of both the songs; but if sung to the second, it retains its own tune. All the stanzas of Number One, with the exception of those commencing "Rise up," are sung during the day.]

NUMBER TWO.

All now for to fetch home
    The summer and the May, O!
For summer is a come, O!
    And winter is a-go.

Up flies the kite,
    And down falls the lark, O!
Un Ursula Bird, she had an old ewe, O!
    And she died in Old Park, O!

Oh, where is St. George?
    Oh, where is he, O?
He's down in his long boat,
    All on the salt sea, O!

Oh, where are those French dogs?
    Oh, where are they, O?
They're down in their long boats,
    All on the salt sea, O!

Oh, where are those French dogs?
    Oh, where are they, O?
They shall eat the grey goose feathers,
    And we will eat the roast, O!

Sir John Barleycorn.

THERE are many versions of this popular song; but the West-country one is believed to be the oldest.

THERE came three men out of the West
　　Their victory to try,
And they have taken a solemn oath
　　Poor Barleycorn should die.

They took a plough, and ploughed him in,
　　And harrowed clods on his head,
And then they took a solemn oath
　　Poor Barleycorn was dead.

There he lay sleeping in the ground
　　Till rain from the sky did fall,
Then Barleycorn sprung up his head,
　　And so amazed them all.

There he remained till midsummer,
　　And looked both pale and wan;
Then Barleycorn he got a beard,
　　And so became a man.

Then they sent men with scythes so sharp
　　To cut him off at knee,
And then, poor little Barleycorn,
　　They served him barbarously.

Then they sent men with pitchforks strong
    To pierce him through the heart,
And like a dreadful tragedy,
    They bound him to a cart.

And then they brought him to a barn,
    A prisoner to endure;
And so they fetched him out again,
    And laid him on the floor.

Then they set men with holly clubs
    To beat the flesh from his bones;
But the miller he served him worse than that,
    For he ground him betwixt two stones.

Oh, Barleycorn is the choicest grain
    That ever was sown on land;
It will do more than any grain
    By the turning of your hand.

It will make a boy into a man,
    And a man into an ass;
It will change your gold into silver,
    And your silver into brass.

It will make the huntsman hunt the fox,
    That never wound his horn;
It will bring the tinker to the stocks,
    That people may him scorn.

    *   *   *   *

It will put sack into a glass,
And claret in the can,
And it will cause a man to drink
Till he can neither go nor stand.

The Barley Mow Song.

This is an old Devonshire song of very ancient date.

HERE'S a health to the barley mow, my brave boys,
Here's a health to the barley mow!
We'll drink it out of the jolly brown bowl,
Here's a health to the barley mow!

Chorus—Here's a health to the barley mow, my brave boys,
Here's a health to the barley mow!

We'll drink it out of the nipperkin, boys,
Here's a health to the barley mow!
The nipperkin and the jolly brown bowl,
Here's a health to the barley mow!

Chorus—Here's a health to the barley mow, my brave boys,
Here's a health to the barley mow!

And so the song goes on; in every verse a new kind of measure or vessel is mentioned, and all are repeated in the third line; so that the last verse may run thus:

We'll drink it out of the ocean, my boys,
Here's a health to the barley mow!

The ocean, the river, the well, the pipe, the hogshead, the half-hogshead, the anker, the half-anker, the gallon, the bottle, the quart, the pint, the half-a-pint, quarter pint, the nipperkin, and the jolly brown bowl.

The Cuckoo.

A CORNISH FOLK SONG.

COMMUNICATED to *Notes and Queries* by the Rev. R. S. HAWKER.

OW of all the birds that keep the tree,
   Which is the wittiest fowl?
Oh, the cuckoo, the cuckoo's the one! for he
   Is wiser than the owl.

He dresses his wife in her Sunday's best,
   And they never have rent to pay;
For she folds her feathers in a neighbour's nest,
   And thither she goes to lay.

He winked with his eye and he buttoned his purse
   When the breeding time began;
For he'd put his children out to nurse
   In the house of another man.

Then his child, though born in a stranger's bed,
   Is his own true father's son;
For he gobbles the lawful children's bread,
   And he starves them one by one.

So of all the birds that keep the tree,
   This is the wittiest fowl;
Oh, the cuckoo, the cuckoo's the one! for he
   Is wiser than the owl.

The Press-Gang.

Sixty years ago this curious West-country ditty was sung not only from the Tamar to the Land's End, but from Barnstaple Bay to the Rame Head. It describes, in rough and ready rhyme, the experiences of a country yokel who was carried off by a press-gang from a wrestling match on Maker Heights, near Plymouth. Now it is almost forgotten by all but very aged memories; and as it is a curious relic of a state of things long passed away, it has been deemed worthy of preservation here. For the copy I am indebted to Mr. Christopher Childs, of Liskeard, who, after a great deal of trouble, succeeded in recovering fragments from old people scattered over Cornwall, and in putting them together in what is evidently a very near approach to its original form. The dialect is mainly that of Devon.

COME listen vather, and mother too,
   And sister Nance, I pray,
   And I'll tell 'ee a passel o' strange things,
Since I've comed home from say.
   I'll tell 'ee a passel o' strange things,
All about the wind and tide,
   How the compass steered as thee never heerd,
And lots o' strange things beside.

       Chorus—Too ral, lal, too ral, &c.

When I went down to Plymouth town,
    There to a inn a hostling,
I went over to Maker Green
    To ha' a scat to wrastling.
A pair o' leatheren breeches was the prize,
    A little the wuss for wear;
Jan Jordan and I drawed two valls a-piece,
    And Dick Simmons comed in for a share.

And jist as the double play had began,
    And Maker clock had nacked six,
Up came a passel o' ugly chaps,
    Wi' lots o' swords and sticks;
They abused Dick Simmons, and darned his eyes,
    And called 'un all sorts o' names.
"Blam 'ee," ses I, "Dick Simmons," says I,
    "They've purfectly spoiled the games."

Then in comed a chap with a great cocked hat,
    That seemed to be the king;
"Blam 'ee," ses I, "if you've a consait,
    Will 'ee stap wi' me into the ring?"
So he turned inside, and I drawed the sword
    Directly out o' his hand,
When a veller behind mur nacked mur down,
    And another he told mur to stand.

Then amang mun all they took mur up,
    And lugged mur down to a boat,
When ses the meister to the men,
    "Let's set the rascal afloat."

But though I begged 'em in good stead—
    And I looked "like anything"—
That they shouldn't top me in the say,
    But send me to serve the king:

There came alang Alias Prowse—
    He was bound for a vurren croos,
And he ran away for a small chield,
    And a devil o' veller he was;—
Then he took mur up both neck and heels,
    And topp'd mur into the say;
But as I always trusted in Providence,
    I wasn't to die thicker way.

Then they took mur out to a gert big ship,
    Which lied far out in the Sound;
The waves did top so cruel high,
    I thought we'd all been drowned,
But I catched hold a rope and climbered up,
    And so I got inside.
Massy upon me, I was so sick,
    I thort I must ha died.

Jist as a nation row began,
    Our ship she jist got out;
The waves did top so cruel high,
    And the wind turned right about.
One cried, "Luff!" another cried, "Tack!"
    And another, "Helm's a-lee!"
But luff and tack, or tack and luff,
    Was all the same thing to me.

Now as we on the ocean sailed,
    We spied a French ship comin';
Our meister beat all hands to quarter,
    And a veller went round a drummin'.
Now I began to call o'er my past life,
    My sinful actions all;
My Lor! ses I, if I should die,
    What would become o' my saul?

Then this French ship up a come,
    And a whole broadside let she;
The sulphur did vly so cruel high,
    I could neither hear nor see.
One got his head a nacked off
    By means o' a cannon ball;
My Lor! ses I, if it's honour to die,
    I don't like sich honour at all.

Then come along the meister of our ship—
    I seem I see the sword o' en—
"Pray then, Jan," ses he, "come along wi' me,
    And I'll warn we'll soon get aboard o' en."
So I vollered about to my meister's heels,
    While t'other men were out vending;
And there I spied a gert French toad,
    And I thought I could make an end o' en.

Then this French veller up a come,
    And showed me his gert long spit;
But I'd a sword made o' a oaken twig,
    And I didn't mind en a bit;

Not though he shet vore, and tho' he shet back,
   And so the toad kept prancing,
Till my oaken twig valled down on his wig,
   Which sot his daylights a dancing.

Then they ordered mur up a-top o' the mast,
   Which I thought was cruel hard,
And there sot a lot of piscy toads
   A-grinning all on the top yards—
Till at last the mast come tumbling down,
   And so did the yards likewise;
And I thought if Maker tower had valled,
   He couldn't have made more noise.

Some valled in the sea, and some on the deck,
   And I had a cruel thump,
When a veller cried, "There's five feet water in hold!"
   So they called all hands to the pump.
So we pumped away till we could hardly stand,
   And we daresn't not to speak,
Till a veller he called out again,
   Sayin', "I've stopped the leak."

Then come aboard all the rest of the crew,
   And drove away all the French vellers;
My meister went vore to a gert big post,
   And hauled down all the French colours.
I went vore to a veller who collared my meister,
   And I beat him black and blue,
From the crown of his head to the sole of his foot,
   Till the rascal called out "murblue."

So now come all you husbandmen
And ostlers, that would vight,
I hope, whenever you're called upon
To maintain old England's right;
For since sich a silly vool as I
Can vight so very well,
Way if ever the French they do come here,
We'll send them all to ——.

The Chapter of Admirals.

This quaint song was originally written to the seventh stanza about 1797, and has been continued by a later hand. The names in italics are those of Western men. The chorus is repeated at the end of each verse.

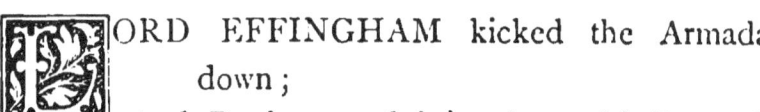ORD EFFINGHAM kicked the Armada down;
And *Drake* was a fighting the world all round.
Gallant *Raleigh* lived upon fire and smoke;
But *Sir John Hawkins's* heart was broke.
Yet, barring all pother,
The one and the other
Were all of them lords of the main.

Sir Humphrey Gilbert was lost at sea;
And frozen to death was poor Willoughby.
Both *Grenville* and Frobisher bravely fell;
But 'twas *Monson* who tickled the Dutch so well.

The heart of a lion had whiskered *Blake;*
And York was a seaman for fighting's sake;
But Montague perished among the brave;
And Spragge was doomed to a briny grave.

To Russel the pride of the Frenchmen struck;
And their ships at Vigo were burnt by Rooke.
But Sir Cloudesley Shovel to the bottom went;
And Benbow fought till his life-shot was spent.

Portobello the Spaniards to Vernon lost;
And sorely disturbed was Hosier's Ghost.
Lord Anson with riches returned from sea;
And Balchin was drowned in the Victory.

Of conquering Hawke let the Frenchmen tell;
And of bold *Boscawen,* who fought so well;
Whilst Pocock and Saunders as brightly shine
In the *Annus Mirabilis* Fifty-nine.

Warren right well for his country fought;
And Hughes, too, did as Britons ought;
Then Parker so stoutly the Dutchmen shook;
And the flower of the French bully Rodney took.

Howe, Jervis, and Hotham did bravely fight,
And the French and Spaniards put to flight;
Whilst the pride of the Dutchmen was put down
By Duncan at glorious Camperdown.

At the Nile our sailors made France to quake;
Copenhagen the Danish fleet did take;
On Victory's deck our Nelson fell;
And Collingwood finished Trafalgar well:

Dundonald the Gama made Speedy work;
Nor Stopford nor Brenton were men to shirk;
Maurice commanded the Diamond crag;
Broke of the Chesapeake struck the flag;

Cockrane the roll of our heroes swells;
Duckworth pressed on through the Dardanelles;
Graves gallantly conquered his peerage claim;
And *Keats* upheld the old Devonshire fame.

Pellew at Algiers made the Dey's sun set;
Navarino will Codrington ne'er forget;
Franklin was lost 'mid the Arctic Seas;
Hall with his "devil ship" scared the Chinese.

Lyons, Napier, *Reynolds*, Keppel, and more,
Have battled all nations on sea or on shore;
When our gallant soldiers needed aid,
Peel dashed on with his Naval Brigade.

'Twere endless to mention each hero's name,
Whose deeds on the ocean our strength proclaim;
Let foemen dare venture to meet us again,
Britain's sons will give proof they are lords of the main.

W. Brendon and Son, Plymouth.

www.ingramcontent.com/pod-product-compliance
Lightning Source LLC
Chambersburg PA
CBHW020845160426
43192CB00007B/785